LAST LAUGH

LAST LAUGH

by

Rex Harley

LONDON
VICTOR GOLLANCZ LTD
1987

First published in Great Britain 1987
by Victor Gollancz Ltd,
14 Henrietta Street, London WC2E 8QJ

British Library Cataloguing in Publication Data
Harley, Rex
  Last laugh.
  I. Title
  823'.914[J]   PZ7
  ISBN 0-575-03920-5

Typeset at The Spartan Press Ltd,
Lymington, Hants
and printed in Great Britain by
St Edmundsbury Press Ltd, Bury St Edmunds, Suffolk

For James
who gave me the typewriter

Contents

Last Laugh

Desmond had been scrubbing the cows for ten minutes with little success. He had been given a bucket, a stiff brush and a tin of scouring powder for good measure, but no-one had told him what to expect when he got there. They didn't tell him anything much. "Dig a hole over there, Des," they said, and only later he'd find out there was a high voltage cable lurking like a fat snake beneath his fork. The other council workmen would have told them where to get off, but Desmond was YTS. The foreman had asked him did he know what that meant. "Youth Training Scheme," he'd said. "No," the foreman said. "It means Do As You're Told and Don't Ask Questions." So he hadn't after that. Not even when they'd said, "Des, go and clean the cows."

There were five of them stuck all by themselves in a field on the edge of the New Town, and they were made of concrete. You had to climb over a fence and scramble down a steep grass bank to get at them. Why anyone should want to make five concrete cows, let alone deposit them in the middle of a field, was more than Desmond could imagine. Equally puzzling was why, once they were there, where no-one could see them unless they were seven foot tall and permanently carried binoculars, someone else should take the trouble to write ARSENAL on their flanks in red spray paint.

Not that he disapproved of the principle: he'd already

received a clip round the ear for adding his name to a bus shelter he was supposed to be cleaning. It was the waste of effort that bemused him. Almost as futile as this constant scrubbing back and forth to get rid of it. The side of the cow was well-lathered by now, as if it had just completed a world record attempt on the mile, but all that had happened to the large letters was a gentle fading of their original brightness. ARSENAL was turning pink. Desmond threw down the brush in disgust.

"Not having much luck?"

The voice came from the other side of the disfigured cow. He peered over its spine to find an old man in a tweed cap looking at him. He was remarkably smart. Besides the cap, he wore a light brown raincoat and his tie was vigorously knotted underneath a protruding Adam's apple. His only concession to the surroundings was a pair of black Wellington boots.

"Where did you come from?" Desmond asked.

"Over the other side of the field."

"I didn't hear you."

"No. Well you wouldn't. You were too busy scrubbing."

Desmond felt a trickle of sweat slide from his forehead to the bridge of his nose. He must have been working harder than he'd realised. He wiped the back of his hand across his head and prodded soap into his eye. It stung. "Hell," he said, and kicked the leg of the nearest cow in frustration. Then he dabbed experimentally at his sore eye with the cuff of his jumper.

"Fancy a cup of tea?" the old man said.

"What?"

"Or coffee if you like. Might even find a few biscuits."

Desmond scanned the horizon for some sign of a café. Had one been airlifted into the field while he was engrossed in the cows, or was the old man simply dotty?

"Well?" the old man said.

"What's your game?" asked Desmond.

"If that's your attitude then you can stay here with those ridiculous animals," he said, and turned on his heel as smartly as rubber boots on wet grass would allow. He had squelched several yards before Desmond's curiosity got the better of him. "Hang on," he called. The old man stopped and waited.

"Do you want to bring your bucket and things?" he said as Desmond caught him up. "Someone might steal them."

"Yes, they might." Desmond had an optimistic glint in one eye. The other was watering badly from the chemicals he had deposited there. "Where we going anyhow?"

"Over there."

Desmond followed the old man's pointing arm and saw, beyond a tall hedge, the corner of a building. "Oh yeah," he said. "What is it?"

"My house."

"I didn't know there was houses out here."

"Only the one," said the old man, "And they'd have knocked that down as well by now, if they'd had the chance." He led Desmond round a patch of boggy ground and through a gap in the hedge.

In front of them was an old red-brick house. It showed its age too: mortar had flaked away from between the bricks and the roof slumped in the middle; certain slates had vanished completely leaving dark, irregular holes; the wooden sills needed more than a lick of paint, and around the doorstep a profusion of weeds held congregation. The old man opened the front door.

Desmond had expected to see buckets in the hallway and damp stains on the wall. In fact the interior was old-fashioned but clean. By the time they reached the kitchen it even felt quite cosy in a strange way. "I more or less live in the kitchen," the old man said, and motioned him into an armchair with a floral cover.

"Hang on." It was only as he was about to make himself comfortable that Desmond realised he had no idea whose house he was in. "Who are you?" he said.

"Mr Greaves, or Walter, whichever you prefer. And you?"

"Desmond. Desmond Brady."

"Tea or coffee, Desmond?"

"Coffee, ta."

Mr Greaves pottered from sink to stove to cupboard and round again, and no more words were exchanged until they both held full mugs. Mr Greaves sipped his coffee thoughtfully. "What do you think of the cows, Desmond?" he said.

"The cows? They're all right I suppose, if you like that sort of thing. But I don't understand them. I mean, are they supposed to be art or something?"

"That's a very good question." He nodded sagely to himself. Desmond felt he needed prompting. "What do you reckon, then?" he said.

Mr Greaves stared hard at the youth in his armchair, as if weighing something up in his mind. "You in a hurry?" he asked. "To get back to your cows?"

"Not really. They might send someone out to see I'm doing my job properly but I doubt it. Not yet anyway.

They're probably too busy playing cards back at the depot."

That seemed to decide the old man. He leaned forward and his face had a strangely fierce look to it. "Seventy-four years ago," he said, "all bar a couple of months, I was born here in this house. It was a working farm then. My father built it up from nothing and by the time he died we had a couple of hundred acres. When you looked out of the windows front and back all you could see was our land and the cattle grazing on it. Where that main road is over there, was nothing but pasture — and cow sheds, of course."

Desmond tried to picture the scene but he had never seen a cow shed at close quarters, and the asphalt road with its tall, yellow street lights had been there as long as he could remember. So had the housing estates that ran along its edges. "What happened?" he asked.

"Very simple. The Government decided it needed somewhere to put all the people they couldn't find houses or jobs for in London. Then a group of planners got hold of a map and drew a circle on it. Soon after that the bulldozers started moving in, and about the same time a couple of men arrived at the front door waving a piece of paper. Compulsory purchase order they called it. It had taken my dad fifty years to build up this farm, and it took them five weeks to steal it off us and start putting up concrete hovels for the newcomers. They've been trying to get the house and this last bit of land for years now. I've been fighting them in the courts but they'll get it eventually. I just hope I'm not around to see it happen. As for the cows, I think they put them up out of spite. So I could look out of my bedroom window and see what they'd taken away from me."

Desmond felt sorry for the old man but he decided to be noncommittal. "Didn't they say something about them being there to remind people of their heritage?" he said.

"Some of us don't need reminding," said Mr Greaves. "You'd better get back to your job before they come round to inspect."

As he left, Desmond felt mysteriously as if he had let the old man down.

When Desmond clocked in at the Maintenance Depot three days later, they were all huddled round the table in a state of suppressed mirth. "Morning, Des," they said. "Seen this?"

Two of them broke ranks so that he could squeeze through. On the table lay a copy of the local newspaper. It had been opened to reveal an article headed VANDALS STRIKE AGAIN.

"What's all this?" Desmond asked.

"Read it," they said.

'During the early hours of Tuesday morning,' it began, 'vandals seriously damaged the sculpture, *Our Rural Past*, commissioned two years ago by the New Town Development Corporation. The sculpture, a group of grazing cows, has been the victim of several attacks but this is the first time it has received such savage attention. A spokesman said that particularly severe damage had been caused to one cow's horns and another had had its left leg broken off at the knee.' "This is a dreadful example of premeditated vandalism," he said. "I am saddened that the youth of our town has so little respect for the environment in which they live." The Development

Corporation is to approach the sculptor, Mr Brian Mansell, with a view to recasting the damaged parts. In the meantime, temporary repairs are to be effected.'

Desmond groaned. "All that time I spent cleaning them," he said.

"I know," said the foreman. "And now you're going to have to go out there again."

"What for?"

"Like it says in the paper: 'temporary repairs'."

Half an hour later, the works van pulled in at the side of the road and Desmond climbed disconsolately from the passenger seat. He collected a roll of wire, plaster of Paris and another bucket from the back of the van; he poured water from a container and closed the back doors again. Then he turned to climb over the fence.

"Hang on," the foreman called. "I'll come with you. Can't fill in your worksheet till I've inspected the damage, can I?" He slammed the driver's door, and the two of them slid down the bank towards the cows.

After a close examination the foreman tutted. "Not much we can do about the odds and ends that have been chipped off, but the horns should be easy enough. You can get started on them. The leg's a bit dodgy but you'll just have to do your best with that. I'll pop back about lunchtime and see how you're getting on." He jotted a few quick notes in his little book and was just closing it when another voice spoke, close enough to make him jump.

"Nasty mess, isn't it?"

Desmond, who was idly stirring the water in the bucket with a stick, looked up to see Mr Greaves standing by the foreman's side. He was patting the nearest cow on the rump. "Do you think you'll be able to repair it?"

The foreman had no intention of hanging around, bandying words with some geriatric in search of casual conversation. "Yes, I should think so," he said curtly.

"Dreadful thing to do," Mr Greaves continued, quite unperturbed by the frosty response. "As a senior citizen it makes me worried to venture out at night. A group of youngsters wielding offensive weapons — well, it could be people they attack next, and the old are particularly vulnerable, you know."

It sounded to Desmond as if he had acquired a wavering croak in his voice since they had last spoken. The effect was to age him by ten years. The foreman nodded to Desmond. "Make a decent job of it. I'll be round later." He scrambled up the bank, got in the van and drove off.

"That your boss?" said Mr Greaves. The croak had gone.

"Yeah."

"Miserable so-and-so, isn't he?"

"You can say that again."

"How long do you think it'll take you?"

Desmond shrugged. "I dunno. There's nothing to hold the leg on, see. I'll probably spend ages moulding it into place and then it'll fall off as soon as my back's turned."

"I tell you what," Mr Greaves suggested. "While you're working out the best way to tackle it, how about doing a small job for me?"

"All right."

For the second time that week they set off towards the house, but just inside the hedge Mr Greaves turned left and stopped outside a small garden shed. "Come in here a minute," he said.

The shed smelt of old grass and engine oil. Mr Greaves pointed to the floor. "That's the problem," he said. "It needs someone with a bit of strength to put it right. My arms haven't got the power they used to."

Desmond bent down and picked up the heavy iron head of the sledgehammer. The wooden haft lay on a bench nearby. There was no damage to either piece; they had simply parted company. "No problem," he said. He looked at the metal head again, then placed it on the bench. He frowned. "When did this happen?"

"A couple of days ago. Why?"

When he turned round, the old man was smiling disarmingly at him. Desmond's mouth fell open. "*You* did the cows," he said.

"It was the leg," said Mr Greaves ruefully. "I had to give it a heavier whack than I'd intended. Next thing I knew, the hammer was flying past my ear and all I was holding was the handle. I made a bit of a botched job of it, didn't I?"

Desmond thought hard for a moment. "When you said you wanted me to do a small job for you — "

"Yes?"

" — you didn't mean — ?"

"Desmond, I wouldn't dream of persuading you to do something criminal."

"No. But if I *wanted* to. I mean, those cows haven't exactly done me any favours."

The two conspirators grinned at each other. "Tonight at eight?" said Mr Greaves. "Between us, I'm sure we can manage to do a decent job."

Maybe Tomorrow

Julie was crying. She had been crying for the past half-hour, and there seemed no tears left in her now. Still she shook, racked with some hidden pain, her legs up under her chin, hands clasping her knees. Backwards and forwards she rocked on her bed, looking steadily at a patch of wallpaper, as if it were the only thing that kept her in touch with the world outside.

Slowly the blurred colours became focused and slowly, too, the rocking eased, until she sat immobile like some strange statue.

Five minutes. Then she took several deep breaths, swung her feet to the floor and stood. The only sound now was the wind brushing the few, scantily-leaved trees outside. She thought back to the violent words and gestures barely an hour before, and the present seemed unreal.

Suddenly she felt very cold. It was December but Julie knew that winter was not the reason. The season simply echoed something that lay deep within her: a freezing of the spirit which grew with every passing month. It would still be there when spring came.

She pulled back the covers of the bed and, without undressing, slid into the one patch of safety and warmth in the whole house.

"Julie Ashcroft."

There was an unnatural silence in the classroom. The fifth form tutor, Mr Foster, was examining her closely from his desk, a faint smile on his lips.

"Earth to Ashcroft. Are you receiving me?"

Julie looked up to see most of the class staring in her direction, several of them giggling.

"Here, sir."

"Good. And let's have you answering first time from now on please, or we'll miss Assembly."

How many times had he called Julie's name? She had no idea; didn't care really. She was still preoccupied with the events of the previous night, trying to make some sense of it all. She'd been doing that for four years now, thinking always that things could not get any worse, when along came some new catastrophe to prove her wrong.

"I said off you go, Julie."

It was Mr Foster again. She must pull herself together. Sarah was hovering by the door, waiting for her.

"Are you all right?"

"Yes thanks, sir. I didn't sleep too well, that's all." There was truth in that.

"OK. Just wondered."

She picked up her bag and left hurriedly. Sarah walked downstairs by her side: silent, receptive, waiting for the right moment.

Sarah was a tall, muscular girl whose physique was accentuated by her choice of clothes. Away from school, she wore bleached jeans and an assortment of outsize sweatshirts; when constrained by the sober uniform of school, she contrived to wear it as brutally as possible. Her blonde hair, once long and the envy of all the mothers in the neighbourhood, had now been cut down to size. And when it had recently been discovered that she needed to wear spectacles, she cheerfully selected the nastiest pair of National Health glasses she could find.

In the same spirit of perversity she had chosen the quietest and least interesting girl in the school as her closest friend. That at least was how Julie regarded the miraculous birth of their friendship when fate had thrown them together in the same class, three years before. Everything that Sarah possessed — assurance, humour and common sense — Julie lacked. The professional cows in the form said she had been selected because she was the one girl who posed no challenge: a weakling whom Sarah could dominate as she wished.

They dumped their bags in the cloakroom and took the long way round to the hall. By the look of it, they were the last two. The Head was standing outside and gave them one of his pained expressions as they passed. Sarah gave him an extra sweet false smile and pulled a face at Julie when they were in the hall. Oh, well. At least twenty minutes of boredom would give her a chance to catch up on lost sleep.

When Break finally came and there was a chance to talk, cold rain streaked the steamy windows: at any moment children of all shapes and ages would come bursting into the classrooms, and privacy would vanish. Rain or no rain, they would have to go outside to talk. Huddled under Sarah's reliable umbrella, they squelched towards the playing field.

At last Julie spoke.

"She's never going to get better, you know."

"Oh, Julie. You don't mean that."

"You reckon?"

"I'm sorry. You mean it now, yes. But that's only because of whatever happened yesterday."

"And three months ago, and in April at my nan's. And that's only this year."

Sarah was silent.

"I mean, sometimes I think 'It's OK, Julie. You're exaggerating. Everybody's mother's a bit crazy'."

"Well, mine is."

"Yes. But she doesn't try to kill herself three times a year."

Julie looked around to see if anyone had heard her. The only people nearby were some first year boys jumping in puddles and kicking muddy water over one another. A podgy boy with messy blond hair backed away from the latest bombardment and tripped into Sarah. She caught him with one hand, looked straight into his eyes and said, loud enough for his friends to hear, "Darling, we really can't go on meeting like this." The other boys laughed and he squirmed, but Sarah had his hand firmly grasped now.

"Parting is such sweet sorrow," she charmed. Loud guffaws from the boys.

Satisfied that he had been sufficiently humiliated, Sarah let go and strolled on as if nothing had happened. Always so cool, thought Julie. If that little squirt had bumped into her she'd probably have sworn at him. You never kept in control of things when you did that. If only she'd remembered that the night before.

Everything had seemed so calm until she'd come home from school to see her mother's face strained and staring at the kitchen window. Or had it really started once she was inside the house and taking off her coat . . .

"Julie!" her mother's voice snapped from the kitchen. "Come here."

Methodically hanging her coat on the peg by its loop — her mother couldn't bear to see the material stretched out of shape — she picked up the tin containing the quiche she had made in Cookery and went into the kitchen.

"What's up, Mum?" she ventured as gently as possible.

"What do you mean? Why should anything be *up*?"

"Well . . . I thought you wanted to see me about something."

"Perhaps I just want to see you. You are my daughter, after all." She sneered the last words with a fine air of reproach, and added, "Though you'd never think so, the way you behave sometimes."

Don't respond, an insistent voice told Julie. But she had been wounded. "What have I done now?"

"What haven't you done, more like. I thought you were supposed to do the washing-up before you went to school this morning?"

"Yes?" Julie stared at her, puzzled. "I did."

Her mother gestured to a teacup and saucer on the draining board. "And what's that, then?"

Julie stared at the cup in disbelief. "But I did all the washing-up before I left . . ."

"But you couldn't have, could you? If I hadn't been suffering from a migraine, *I'd* have done it — properly. But I was in bed, so your dad was kind enough to bring me a cup of tea."

"It's *your* cup? Well, how was I supposed to know about that? Dad didn't tell me, and anyway — " She stopped and bit her tongue.

Her mother glared at her. Julie watched the muscles on her hands start to writhe. The veins in the back of her hands were raised in ridges spreading out from the knuckles to the wrists: an old woman's hands.

"Anyway — what?" she said.

"Nothing."

"Anyway, you wouldn't have fetched it even if you did know. That's what you mean, isn't it?"

"Christ, Mum. It's only a cup. I'll wash it up now if you like."

Julie moved towards the draining board.

"Don't you swear at me," her mother snarled, and slapped her hand away as it was reaching for the cup. "And answer my question. You wouldn't have fetched it, would you?"

"What?"

"The cup!"

All right, Julie thought, have it your own way. "No," she said quietly and deliberately. "I wouldn't."

She waited patiently for the stream of hatred she knew would be unleashed at her. But her mother merely said, "What have you got there?" and pointed at the large, round tin that Julie had placed on the work unit.

Julie eyed her mother suspiciously. "It's the quiche we made in Cookery. Why?"

"Quiche! In the middle of winter? Let's see it anyhow."

Julie took off the lid and held out the tin for her mother's inspection.

"Huh," she snorted. "What mark did you get for this?"

"Nine out of ten," Julie retorted, her voice arrogant though she had not intended it.

"Give it here, then."

Hesitantly she began to hand it over. At the moment the tin was transferred, and she felt her finger tips brush against the cold skin of her mother's, Mrs Ashcroft pulled her hands away and the tin fell. It landed on its side, discharging its contents upside-down onto the kitchen floor. Julie's worn patience finally snapped.

"You bitch!" she spat at her mother. "You stupid bitch!"

"How dare you!" Her mother's hand slapped hard against her cheek. Julie fought the urge to hit back. She mustn't. She mustn't.

"Go to your room," her mother was shouting. "Just wait till I tell your father."

"All right," Julie shouted back. "You tell him. Tell him you deliberately ruined my cookery; tell him you're never happy unless you're making me miserable; tell him . . ." Her voice was wavering now with the tears that threatened to drown her words. "Tell him what a cow you really are, and then ask him why he married you in the first place."

She slammed out of the kitchen and grabbed her coat roughly from the peg.

"Julie," her mother called. "Julie!"

Ignoring the strident yells, she flung open the front door and walked, head down, to the gate. She had no idea how long it would take to walk off her anger but one thing she knew for certain: she could not step back inside that house until she had. The way she felt now, anything could happen and it was bound to be violent. Once the corner of the street had been turned, she stopped. There was no point in wandering aimlessly. The best thing was to fix a destination and stick to it; that way at least she felt she was going somewhere. The most obvious was the town centre so she set off in that direction.

Darkness had already settled on the surrounding houses and street lamps found their echo in lighted living rooms. Curtains had been drawn in many, but the occasional window was still uncovered. Every now and then Julie paused to peer into other people's small worlds and tried to guess what happened there. In one front room two children were watching television, clutching porcelain mugs too large for their fingers. Each time they lifted the mugs to drink, they spilled a little over the edge. Julie imagined how her mother would react to that!

Where was their mother? In the kitchen making their tea, probably. Or maybe they didn't have a mother, or she was round at a neighbour's while Dad did the work. People thought they knew what went on in others' homes, but they never did; domestic truths were hidden from the gaze of strangers.

As she watched, a young woman of about twenty came into the room and, ignoring the children, walked over to the curtains. Julie turned quickly away before the woman caught her nosing into their privacy.

She walked and walked for nearly an hour, knowing that by the time she returned her father would be home. But as she neared the house, all thoughts of what he might be waiting to say to her were scattered by the vehicle parked outside: it was an ambulance.

Though her legs ached she ran the last fifty yards. The front door was open and there was no-one to be seen.

Then her father appeared with a small suitcase in one hand. His face was pale and he walked in a daze. Behind him came an ambulance man.

"Dad," she called and ran up to him, gasping.

He looked up and saw her. But it was several seconds before he spoke. "Where . . . have you been?" he asked slowly.

"What's happened? Where's Mum?"

He seemed unaware that she had failed to answer his question. "In the ambulance," he said. "I'm going with her to the hospital. You wait here. I'll phone you later."

"But what happened?"

The ambulance man moved diplomatically away and waited by the privet hedge. Mr Ashcroft shook his head. "Not now. I'll tell you later."

"But she . . ."

"Yes. It's all right. She'll be OK."

He squeezed her shoulder, and she watched him walk awkwardly to the ambulance. The door was opened for him and he climbed in without a backward glance. The ambulance pulled away and, as it left the road, Julie heard the siren begin to wail. She turned to go into the house, and only then did she realise that the windows on the ground floor were all wide open. In the house next door a lace curtain twitched back into place. Julie knew it would be the only sign of neighbourly concern shown towards her or her family. She entered her home. The smell of gas still hung in the hallway.

Eighteen hours later, in the fresh air of a rain-swept playground, the ghost of that smell returned unbidden to her nostrils. She turned away from Sarah.

"You don't have to tell me any more if you don't want to," Sarah prompted.

"I want to but I . . . can't somehow. I'm sorry. Maybe later."

"Yeah. OK." Sarah kicked at the edge of a large puddle and they walked on in silence past the tennis courts, the nets long stored away, rain lashing the net posts.

Julie knew she would have to talk about it at some time, if only to exorcise the evil spirits of the night. But not now: this was the wrong place and the wrong time; and the words still clotted in her throat.

When Julie arrived home at four fifteen, the house was empty. On the dining room table lay a note:

Julie —
Gone visiting. Back about five. A cup of tea would be welcome.
Love, Dad.

Julie folded the piece of paper neatly into four and knife-edged the creases with her finger-nails, then replaced it on the table. She wandered through to the living room. A quick flick through the buttons on the television told her there was nothing worth watching, so she just kicked off her shoes and sat curled up in the large armchair.

The room, scene of so many bitter arguments, seemed ill-suited to silence. The noises from the street outside were muffled and indistinct. Even the electric clock operated so quietly that its ticking heartbeat could not be heard. It made Julie feel uncomfortable — but not so horribly uncomfortable as the night before.

Waiting for her father to return had been bad enough: his brief phone call from the hospital had told her nothing, except that his voice sounded more distant than the two miles between them. But when he returned, the full horror of what had happened returned with him.

Before his key had finished turning in the lock, she had been in the hallway to greet him.

"Hello, Dad."

When he replied his words were devoid of all emotion. "Hello, Julie." Her heart fell.

"Dad, are you angry with me?"

He took off his coat and threw it over the banister. He smelled of the night outside and the bus ride home. Also on his breath Julie could smell drink; not much — he'd probably had a pint at the most — but in the antiseptic cleanliness of the house it was as obvious as laughter at a funeral.

He walked past her and into the living room without answering. Apprehensively she followed. He did not sit down but stood with his shoulders hunched, staring at the gas fire. When finally he spoke, he continued to look fixedly away from Julie's face. "Why did you do it?"

"Me? What did I do?"

"Don't make me any angrier than I am, Julie. Your mother's staying in hospital at least until tomorrow evening for observation, but she was able to talk before I left. She told me what you said to her."

Julie wanted desperately to get close to her father, to shatter this terrible coldness before she tried to explain; but she knew he would not let her near.

"Oh," she said despondently.

"Is that all you've got to say?"

"What else *can* I say? I'm sorry for what happened, but it wasn't my fault."

"What the hell do you mean?" Mr Ashcroft turned to face his daughter. His eyes were beads of compressed anger and hurt.

Julie began to move away, out of reach of that overwhelming coldness. "Please," she begged. "Don't look at me like that. It *wasn't* my fault."

Her father grabbed her by the shoulders and pulled her round to face him again.

"You look at me when I'm talking to you. What you said to your mother would have been unforgivable at any time, but when you know how ill she is . . ."

"I didn't mean what I said. I'm sorry. But she pushed me so hard. She wanted me to say it."

"You uncaring — "

"No, listen. She wants me to, because when I explode it makes her feel in control; like she's not really cracking up, it's me. It makes her feel better. And it's always worse when you're not around. I don't suppose she told you she tipped my cooking on the floor?"

"She told me you lost your temper because of some- thing that was a straightforward accident."

"Accident? Accident my arse!"

"Julie!"

"Oh, not you as well! Why shouldn't I swear? It's about the only way I've got left to let my feelings out. She reckons she's the only one in this house who's got any feelings. We're all supposed to worry about the state of *her* health, but what about yours and mine?"

"Julie, if you don't stop — "

"No! I spend all my time listening to what other people

tell me. Why don't people listen to me? What I'm trying to tell you is that she does all this to punish me. God knows what for. Probably just for being alive. No . . ."

Sudden realisation made her stop. She weighed up the thought that had struck her. "I know why she does it. She's scared, isn't she? Scared that I'm taking you away from her; that you love me more than you love her. It's her way of making you care."

One moment her father was still, the next his hand was snaking towards her head. The blow was clean and hard, thundering against her temple. She stumbled and fell, crashing against the armchair.

Out of the stinging silence came his voice, blurred and frightened. "Oh, God. Julie. I'm sorry, Julie. I'm sorry. I'm sorry."

He tried to help her to her feet, but she shrugged away his hand and pulled herself up. Slowly, deliberately, she walked around the chair to the door.

"Julie . . ."

He was devastated and there were no words of comfort in her.

Long after she had cried herself to sleep, the light in the living room remained on.

Maybe he'd sat in this same armchair Julie now occupied, wondering what to do next while his wife and daughter lay in separate rooms; separate worlds, and he was a stranger to both of them.

Julie checked the clock: twenty to five. Ten minutes more and she'd make the tea. The routine preparations would be a welcome change from thought.

At five past, her father returned. She could tell straight away that he was nervous of her. She smiled tentatively. "I've made your tea, Dad. Oh, and thanks for the note."

Mr Ashcroft attempted a smile of his own. "Oh . . . that's OK. Did you . . . Was everything all right at school?"

"Mm. Not too bad. How about your day?"

"I went into work this morning, then in the afternoon I went over to the hospital."

Julie stayed silent.

"They told me she'd be coming home tomorrow. They're keeping her in tonight, just to be certain."

Julie handed him the teacup. He placed it carefully on the nearest worktop and took her hands in his. "Look, I know I can't make up for what happened last night. I suppose we both reached the end of our tether, that's all."

She leaned her head on his shoulder. The coarse-textured jacket pressed hard against her cheek, deluding her for a moment that the burning sensation she felt was not really the onset of tears. And then suddenly they came, shaking her whole body in a violent spasm of crying. For more than a minute her father held her tightly, stroking her hair. Softly his words brushed her cheek:

"It's all right, Julie. Really it is. Things will be all right."

How many times had he said that before, and how many times had he been proved wrong? This time something — small, very small, but something felt different. She could not say why, but it was the very calmness of his voice that frightened her.

From her bed in the corner, Julie breathed in the darkness of the room and tried to get to sleep. It should have been easy: her eyes were sore from tiredness and crying. But just as it seemed she was crossing the narrow border between drowsiness and sleep some wakeful reflex pushed her eyes open again. Normally when this happened, she could fool her mind into thinking of nothing long enough to drift over that shifting boundary. But not now. Tomorrow was Saturday — no need to worry about school — and that left her free to worry about her mother's return.

Mr Ashcroft had decided, and Julie had agreed, that they should both make the journey to the hospital. It would not be a new experience, of course. Her life and her father's had been subject to the ebb and flow of Mrs Ashcroft's illness for a long time. The process had become so repetitious it was difficult to say in what order events had occurred. Even the suicide attempts themselves had become confused in Julie's mind.

Forced to survey the past in this way, Julie realised that each time she did so the moments which seemed important were always different, probably because the process had been so gradual. Someone had to work out the point at which it all began, and it seemed impossible to Julie that her mother could look at herself long enough to find it. Maybe if they all tried they could discover that tiny shift of mind which caused the final turbulence.

Ten years ago, five even, they had been a happy, healthy family and her mother had looked so young. When the two of them were out together people had genuinely mistaken them for sisters, for both had the same wavy, auburn hair and the same grey eyes and oval face; the little girl pretty, the mother beautiful. Even as a young girl, Julie had been aware of the way men regarded her mother admiringly, jealous of her father's good fortune. No doubt her memory was idealising the past. It remained true, nevertheless, that the spiteful, emaciated woman in the hospital had been attractive once, and loving. What was worse, Julie had loved her.

Then the first of the phobias had descended, and soon Mrs Ashcroft was accumulating them as a collector gathers antique stuffed birds and large, brightly-coloured butterflies displayed under glass. Fear of loud noises; fear of dust; fear of open spaces, fear of growing old; fear of dying — fear of living.

Maybe this time, together, they could find a solution. Maybe, as her father had said, everything really would be all right. Julie lay back and closed her eyes again.

Maybe tomorrow morning.

The Ashcrofts hadn't owned a car for several years; it had been too expensive a luxury. Julie and her father walked most places, biked or caught the bus, and on the rare occasions that Mrs Ashcroft travelled any distance she did so by taxi. Thus, they arrived at the hospital by bus and left it in a taxi. The journey home was made in silence.

Julie was not surprised. Her mother managed to poison the kindest of acts. They had tried to show her genuine consideration and, for all the good it had done, they might as well have stayed at home and let her come back in an ambulance. Julie felt stupid and redundant.

The war of silence continued until Mrs Ashcroft had been re-installed in the house. Then, from the security of her bed, she spoke.

"I want you to know," she said with exaggerated calm,

"that I regard what happened as over and done with. I don't say it will be easy to forget but I shall try."

She stared expectantly at Julie.

"I'm sorry, Mum," she replied on cue. There was no trace of irony in her voice. She had spent the whole of the bus journey rehearsing.

Her father smiled at her. Mrs Ashcroft turned her face sideways slightly, so she appeared to be looking at the top of the wardrobe. Julie leaned forwards and kissed her on the cheek. The smell of heavily-applied perfume made her choke. It was difficult for her not to show the intense physical disgust she felt by pulling quickly away from her mother, but she controlled the urge, beat it down until she left this suffocating sickroom. It shouldn't be long now. She'd delivered her lines, and any moment now her father would say:

"Off you go, Julie. I'd like a few words with your mum."

"OK, Dad." A small half-smile in the direction of the bed and exit through bedroom door, up-stage left.

Once outside, she walked far enough away not to be heard, then hit the wall with the side of her clenched fist. Why had she contributed to that ridiculous charade? Did she really feel guilty for what had happened? Was it her fault; her place to apologise? Don't even think about it, she told herself. It will do no good.

She shut herself in her room, intending to read for the rest of the morning, but her mother had other ideas. Roman emperors, Julie remembered from a distant History lesson, were in the habit of holding court from their beds, ordering all and sundry to attend to their pleasure and answer their every whim. This was the time-honoured example her mother followed for the rest of that day. Lunchtime brought a brief respite but the afternoon produced yells and bleated instructions that worked on Julie's nerves like a series of electric shocks.

By three o'clock, as she tried to learn a piece of French homework, she was stopping every two minutes to listen for the summons down the landing. When it failed to materialise, she was able, at last, to concentrate on irregular verbs. She might even remember a few of them:

"Je vais, tu vas, il/elle va, nous allons, vous allez, ils vont," she repeated.

"Je suis allé(e), tu es . . ."

"Julie."

"What?"

"Julie!"

Oh, hell. Now what did she want? Julie threw the book on the bed and went to answer her mother's call. She knocked on the door and pushed it open. Immediately her mother's fingers began to twitch and her face to look more drawn and heavily-lined. A good performance today, Julie thought. You're on form.

"Yes, Mum?"

"I've been calling for the last five minutes. What have you been doing?"

"Reading." It was best to keep the answers short, not to provoke her any further.

"That's about as much as you care for me, isn't it? Anything could have happened and you'd have been buried in your book. I want to see your father."

"Why don't you call him then?"

"I have, and don't try to be clever with me. We all know how clever you are, madam. And so you should be, all the time you spend on your work instead of looking after me."

"Yes, Mum. He must be out in the garage. I'll go and fetch him."

"And you can take that tray down while you're at it."

"Yes, Mum." She picked up the tray, determined not to let her hands shake with the fury she felt. She opened the door.

"And Julie — "

"Yes, Mum?"

"Take that insolent tone out of your voice, or I'll tell your father to keep you in as a punishment."

It's true, she thought as the door closed behind her. Sarah had once said there was humour in everything, however bleak it seemed. She hadn't believed her then, thinking it had been said just to cheer her up. But here she was, walking down the stairs, giggling so much the cup kept nearly sliding off the tray. '. . . Keep you in as a punishment' — she'd been imprisoned in that house for years, and her mother hadn't even realised. Good old Mum. She didn't even know what was happening in her own house if it didn't centre round her.

As she had suspected, her father was tinkering with his bike.

"You've just had a summons, Dad."

"Hm?"

"Not for speeding or loitering with intent. Probably for not putting enough sugar in the tea."

"Oh. Thanks."

"Be warned. She may have had enough Valium to knock out a herd of buffalo, but she's pretty snappy all the same."

Mr Ashcroft sighed. "I wish you wouldn't joke about it."

"Sorry. But what's that old saying? If you didn't laugh, you'd cry."

She realised suddenly that if she wasn't careful, that's just what she would do. One minute she'd been giggling, and now she was having to fight back the tears.

"I know, love." He squeezed her hand as she passed. "Why don't you go out for a while? Go and see Sarah or something."

"Thanks. Yes, I think I will. When do you want me back?"

"Oh, not for a couple of hours or so. See you later."

"OK, Dad."

There were times when she was surprised how clearly he understood her feelings. Before going back into the house, she leaned over and kissed him on the cheek. The gesture was the same as the one she had earlier made to her mother; the feelings behind it could not have been more different.

"Draw the curtains, David. It's getting dark already, and cold."

Mr Ashcroft obediently closed them. The room was lit only by a small bedside lamp which allowed cold shadows to gather untouched in the corners. He sat on the bed at the edge of its circle of light, and waited to hear what his wife had called him for. But, though she adjusted the bedcovers to make herself more comfortable, she said nothing. Mr Ashcroft cleared his throat and it sounded unnecessarily loud.

"Julie's gone out for a while," he said. "She's pretty

upset about things, you know, even if she doesn't show it."

Mrs Ashcroft turned away. Her profile in the light showed the high cheekbones and sunken skin clearly.

"Look, Margaret, I know you think she doesn't like you but it's not that simple. She does care but you do make it rather hard for her at times. It's only natural . , ,"

"David, if you don't mind, I think I'd like to sleep for a while."

Mr Ashcroft sat where he was. "I know what you're trying to do," he said calmly, "but I'm afraid things *need* to be talked about, and just now we need to talk about Julie."

"Oh, do we?" she demanded. "In that case, you'll be pleased to know that's the very reason I asked you to come up here."

Mr Ashcroft was baffled. "But you just . . ."

"There's no point in discussing it if you start off by thinking she's upset. It's quite obvious what she feels and she doesn't try very hard to hide it, but of course she's been lying to you again, hasn't she, in her usual sly way? If you could have seen her up here ten minutes ago: she positively gloats over me being unwell. I mean, I worry about her. I don't like to use the word but she seems almost sadistic at times."

"There are two sides to every coin," her husband remarked.

Mrs Ashcroft was surprised by her husband's bluntness. Words, for once, deserted her.

"I just think," he continued, "that it would help if we all thought of each other a bit more in this family."

"And *I* don't. Is that what you're saying?"

What was the point of this, Mr Ashcroft thought. All they did was go round in circles. But he could not give up yet. "Listen, Margaret," he said gently. "We have a chance. I was going to wait to tell you but now seems as good a time as any. I've been talking to Dr Lambert, and he says there's the possibility of a vacancy at one of the day centres.

"I'm mad, that's what you're saying! What will you do: have me certified? That'd get me off your hands nicely, wouldn't it?"

Mr Ashcroft hit the bed with his fist. "No," he said. "I'm doing nothing of the sort. Don't you see? I'm trying to find a way of making things work between us." He tailed off and shrugged his shoulders sadly.

Mrs Ashcroft's mouth was a tight, straight line. She watched her husband flounder for a moment, then said, "There *is* a way of making things work."

"How?" he asked helplessly.

"Get Julie to go and stay with your mother for a while. I'm sure she wouldn't mind having her. Then we'd have time to be together more, a chance to sort things out by ourselves, without her getting in the way."

Her husband stared at her in shaken disbelief. In her single-minded attempt to blame Julie, she had ignored every word he'd said.

"What then?" he asked quietly. "What happens when she comes back? Have you thought of that?"

Mrs Ashcroft brushed the question aside irritably. "Oh, I don't know. But at least she wouldn't have a chance to mess things up from the very beginning. You don't understand. She makes me worse. I'd be all right if she didn't treat me the way she does. You should see her sometimes while you're still at work, then you wouldn't be so quick to jump to her defence all the time."

Concern was slipping steadily away from Mr Ashcroft the longer he listened, like the hero in an old film whose fingers are losing their grip on the cliff edge as he looks despairingly down at the pointed rocks and crashing waves below. Soon the woman in the bed would not matter; what happened to her would be of no interest to him. She was already too far away.

"Are you really suggesting," he said, when his wife's tirade had ended, "that Julie is responsible for your illness?"

"You're not listening, are you? I said she makes me worse."

"But she's not responsible for it being there in the first place?"

If Mrs Ashcroft knew the answer, she seemed unwilling to give it. Her fingers picked at the edge of the blanket. "I just think it would be easier . . ."

"Is it Julie's fault that you're ill?" her husband demanded.

"No, but she makes things worse." She looked at him imploringly and tears began to form, glistening on the rim of her eyes. "Please, David. Just for a few weeks so we can spend some time together. By ourselves, David, please."

The tears began to flow.

Mr Ashcroft stood and picked up the empty teacup from the bedside table. Even in the ten minutes he had been there the room had visibly darkened.

When he was half-way to the door the woman behind him screamed. "You don't care, do you? You don't even care what happens to me. You're as bad as her, that little bitch; you make a fine pair. You wouldn't have been sorry if I'd died."

Mr Ashcroft stood looking down at the carpet. He could not bring himself to turn round; he did not want to see any more what his wife had become. He reached for the door, opened it and stepped out of the room. The voice from the bed pierced his back.

"Next time," it shrilled. "Next time I'll do it properly."

The door closed.

Mr Ashcroft walked stone-faced downstairs.

Sarah's bedroom was twice the size of a broom-cupboard, and nearly as cluttered, but on a cold winter's afternoon that made it a comfortable place to be. Once a space had been cleared between the door and the bed and the door closed, everything had to be piled back in its original position in order for anyone to sit down. There was one window which faced the door and gave a view out onto several narrow back gardens and an overgrown footpath. The other walls were plastered with posters, like hoardings, and even the ceiling sported a male model, who could be seen best when lying in bed. The remainder of the decorations consisted of books, magazines, clothes, records and a chest of drawers.

No-one was allowed in the room except by personal invitation, and that included Sarah's mother. Everyone, Sarah argued, needed one small space to call their own, and when the Social Studies teacher had given it a term — Defensible Space — she was quick to seize on this proof of her belief. There was now a notice on the outside informing would-be trespassers that: Violation of Sarah's Defensible Space is Punishable by Extreme

Violence. The notice was largely unnecessary: both her younger brother and father stayed as far away from it as possible, and her mother hunted for dust in more accessible corners of the house.

The room exuded an atmosphere of security, and Julie found she was able to relax more quickly sitting in a tiny clearing on Sarah's bed than anywhere else she knew. Sarah herself preferred the floor, sitting propped against the chest of drawers with her knees up under her chin.

Although they had been in the room only half an hour, Julie had already confided the rest of the week's events to the pensive figure on the floor. Sarah had said very little, and Julie was grateful for that, but now the serious business was over she pointed to the picture on the ceiling.

"What do you think of him?" she asked.

Julie twisted her head round to get the best angle for examining it. "Well, he's better than anything at school," she said at last.

"You really are an expert at understatement, aren't you?" Sarah grinned. "He's fantastic. Look at those pectorals."

"His what?"

"His pectorals. Never mind. Sometimes I forget you're an ignorant non-scientist. They're his muscles. Well, his chest muscles to be accurate."

Julie looked back at the object of her friend's admiration. "I don't know how you get away with it," she said. "If I stuck *any* pictures on the walls at home, my mum would throw a fit — never mind nude men."

"Semi-nude," Sarah corrected. "You can only see his

top half. Even my mum draws the line somewhere: in his case, about an inch above the bum."

Julie's eyes widened, then she burst out laughing. "You mean there was more of him before you stuck him up there?"

"Oh yes." Sarah raised her eyebrows and smiled knowingly. "Plenty more!"

"Go on? Where did you get the picture from then?"

"Aha!" Sarah stood up, and stretched her legs as far as the surrounding objects would allow to dispel the cramp she could feel coming. She knelt down again next to Julie and reached a hand beneath the bed. "One of the great advantages of having a room like a tip is that nobody else can find the things that I want to keep hidden."

She withdrew a magazine and dropped it in Julie's lap, then pushed aside a couple of jumpers and sat next to her on the bed.

"I threw away the rest of the guy on the ceiling. Somehow his bottom half lost some of its appeal after I'd been forced to guillotine his torso. But there's plenty more in there. Go on," she prompted. "Feast your eyes on the assembled talent."

Julie felt silly. She wanted to look inside, but Sarah's eagerness made her nervous. The man on the cover was harmless enough. He leered out glassy-eyed and far too arrogantly to be attractive. Doing her best to appear nonchalant, she flipped through the glossy pages and was uncertain whether to be shocked or amused. Most of the models had clearly been chosen for reasons other than their faces and displayed their assets generously, confident of female approval. Julie found them faintly preposterous.

"Do they really turn you on?" she asked at length.

Sarah peered over at the page she was examining. "Hm. Not him," she said. "He's a bit of a wally, isn't he? But one or two of them, yes."

"Which ones?"

Sarah took the magazine and leafed further on. "This one: the one on the ceiling. And him, though he's a bit old."

She passed it back to Julie for her to see. Julie scrutinised the man on the page. He was in his mid-thirties, with short, dark hair and a moustache, and the first photograph showed him in a business suit, white shirt and striped tie, relaxing in an armchair, a glass of wine on a small table at his side. In the space of eight photographs he gradually removed the clothes he was wearing but even the final photographs in the sequence had none of the coarse banality of the others in the magazine. They were not overtly sexual, as much as sensual, hinting at a calmness and control in the man that gave depth to his attractive face and body.

"Thought so," Sarah chuckled in her ear.

"What?"

"I thought you'd like him."

"Why?" Julie's voice had a defensive edge which surprised her. "Why should I like him?"

"Oh, no reason in particular."

Sudden footsteps on the stairs outside heralded a brisk knock on the door. Sarah reacted promptly. "Yes?" she called, simultaneously closing the incriminating magazine and sliding it back under the bed. The door opened a short way, and a hand appeared with a mug of coffee.

45

"You'll have to take them separately," Sarah's mother called back from the landing. "I can't get the door open. There's a packet of biscuits too."

"Oh thanks, Mum." Sarah stepped carefully over scattered oddments and her mother passed the coffee and biscuits through the narrow gap, like a zoo keeper feeding buns through the bars of a chimp cage.

"That's the lot," she said, but the hand advanced a little further, enough to manage a restricted wave. "Hello, Julie. I don't know if I'll see you before you go, but I don't want to seem unfriendly. I presume I'm waving in the right direction." The hand withdrew. "You are sitting on the bed, aren't you?"

Julie laughed. "Yes, I am. Thank you for the coffee, Mrs Carter. I'm sure I'll see you sometime soon."

"I wouldn't depend on it, dear," her voice came back. "Things go in that room that are never seen again. It's like a miniature version of the Bermuda Triangle. Won't be long now before some poor unsuspecting soul disappears under all that rubbish, and it might be you."

Sarah pulled a face at the door. "Thank you, mother. Sarcasm is the lowest form of wit, but thanks for the drinks anyway."

"And wit is the highest form of intelligence. Don't mention it; you're welcome." Her slippered feet could be heard descending the stairs triumphantly.

"Mothers!" Sarah snorted. "Who'd have 'em?"

"True, but I'll do you a swap if you like." Julie took the proffered cup of coffee. "Thanks. Just for a week or so, of course. That'd be long enough to make you appreciate your mother."

"I know. I was only joking."

"Yes, but I wasn't. I really do wish someone else could see how impossible my mother is. When I tell you, it sounds like I'm exaggerating; if you could see what goes on."

Sarah resumed her seat by the chest of drawers. She took several sips from her coffee then asked, quite casually, "Do you hate your mother?"

Julie knew it was a serious question and that it deserved a considered answer. She thought hard before replying.

"I don't know. I honestly don't know. I suppose, if I'd answered off the top of my head, I'd have said yes. But now I'm not sure. I hate what she's become, I know that. I hate the illness and what it's done to her. Once I could see the difference, between her and her illness, I mean; but now, most of the time, they seem one and the same. She's not my mother any more."

She was still searching for a clearer answer. Finally she shook her head and said, "I don't know if I hate her, but I know I don't love her any more."

"Not now maybe — "

"Not now, not ever. Its no good. I'll never be able to forget what she's done."

"What about your dad?"

"What? How I feel about him, you mean?"

Sarah nodded slowly.

"I don't know. There are times when I feel really close to him, and there are other times when he shuts me out — that's when I worry about him the most. He tries to be so calm and controlled but inside he's falling apart. And I don't think he's got anyone else he can talk to, not like I have."

Sarah stuck out a foot and kicked Julie on the knee. "Don't give me compliments," she said. "They'll only go to my head."

Julie tried to smile, but the cloak of despair had begun to wrap itself around her once more. Sarah stood and put her hand on Julie's shoulder.

"Listen. If ever you need to get away from things, you know you can come round here, don't you? I mean *any* time, even if it's the middle of the night. Mum and Dad won't ask any questions. They like you, you know."

Julie looked up gratefully at her friend's anxious face.

"More to the point," Sarah continued, "*I* like you and I don't want to see you get hurt."

How can you get hurt, Julie thought, when you're so numb you can no longer feel pain?

Mr Ashcroft and Julie had their tea in the living room. This in itself was something of a special occasion; it was an unwritten rule that meals of any sort should be confined to the kitchen or the dining room. As there were only the two of them downstairs, however, Mr Ashcroft suggested that they might take the risk.

"How is she then?" Julie had asked.

"Oh, she's quietened down a bit now," he'd answered. "Best not to disturb her. I think she's fallen asleep."

Julie couldn't remember the last time they'd had tea in front of the television but she seemed to recall they'd been watching *Dr Who* at the time. The programme on now was one of those ridiculous game shows where everyone gets very excited at the prospect of winning a month's holiday in Miami, and leaves the show with a cuddly toy.

Julie and her father said very little but it was a

comfortable silence, companionable even. The gas fire hissed gently, the curtains and doors were firmly closed against the winter evening, and the contestants on the television came and went. Julie even enjoyed watching the adverts. It always amazed her how much money and ingenuity went into persuading people that their lives would be incomplete without a particular brand of toilet paper or bleach. Today the products most in evidence seemed to be cars and gravy, and the families in all of them looked exactly the same: mum, dad and young children beaming at each other with absolute conviction.

And then a disturbing idea occurred to her. That image of herself and her parents, the one she had so nostalgically conjured up the night before. Had they ever really been like that, or was she confusing them with these ideal families on television? Surely not. That was like saying that you couldn't separate fantasy from reality. Then she remembered the thousands of women who sent knitted babyclothes to pregnant housewives in the long-running soap operas on TV and radio — only they weren't pregnant, or housewives, but professional actresses who had no idea what to do with two hundred-weight of bootees, except give them away to charity.

Stop it, she said to herself. *You* can tell the difference; that's the important thing. The family you remember is *your* family. But she was no longer certain.

"Julie?"

"Hm?"

"You were in a world of your own there for a moment. Do you want anything more to eat?"

"Sorry, Dad. No thanks."

"I think I'll have another piece of toast," he pondered. "It's hungry work watching this rubbish."

His plate had been resting on the arm of the chair. As Mr Ashcroft stood up he caught it with his elbow, sending it flying and scattering a shower of toast crumbs over the carpet.

"Tut, tut. Slap your wrists," Julie scolded him. "Hang on, I'll get a dustpan and brush."

He pushed her gently but firmly back into her seat. "You'll do no such thing," he said. "Let them stay there. No housework allowed at the weekend."

They looked at each other like a pair of guilty children and laughed.

Julie undressed slowly. The warmth of the living room and several hours of doing nothing at all had made her pleasantly tired. It was good to feel muscles relaxed and adrenalin slowed down. She put on the striped pyjamas which she'd insisted on buying for the winter, despite her mother's disgust at their lack of shape and femininity. It had done little good to point out that the pretty negligée favoured by Mrs Ashcroft was certain to freeze every extremity of her body. Julie also knew that had *she* chosen the negligée, and not her mother, it would immediately have been denounced as too revealing and totally impractical.

During the evening Julie had become aware of an annoying spot on her chin. Determined to attack it before going to bed, she sat down at the dressing table and leaned towards the mirror, her head twisted sideways and her chin thrust out. It took several goes to get rid of the spot and, by the time she had finished, it looked worse than when she had begun. How perverse, she thought, to make a large, red blotch which stung her face, just to be rid of a tiny blemish. Was that vanity or determination?

She studied her face in the mirror. It was certainly more stubborn than good-looking. The boys at school remained largely unimpressed by it, but then most of the boys she knew were only impressed by themselves. As for boys outside school, she simply didn't know any: the situation never arose. And anyway, she wouldn't have the heart to bring them home to meet the family.

Now she thought about it, though, the idea of a boyfriend definitely had its merits: more opportunity of escaping from the house for one thing. She could do with a little bit of love and affection as well. Just to be held and hugged in a man's arms . . . Well, there you are, she thought. You said it. A *man's* arms. Fat chance of that. You'd end up with one of those randy fifth year boys who try to pull your knickers down before bothering to ask your name.

As she put out the light and climbed into bed, she remembered the man in the magazine. Perhaps she should have asked Sarah if she could have those photographs. It would have been worth the initial embarrassment to be able to look at him again now: strong and in control like a man should be.

Oh, Julie, don't be ridiculous, she thought. You're starting to think like the heroine in a Mills and Boon romance. He wasn't a real man, any more than the families in the adverts were real families. He was just a professional poser who made a living by taking off his clothes.

Down the landing a bedroom door closed: her father's probably. To think that her parents now slept in separate rooms. Whose decision had that been, or was it by mutual consent? She suddenly wondered when they had last made love and, immediately after, wondered why she had never considered that before.

From the darkness of her bed, the click of the door prompted a sudden picture of her mother and father standing in her room when she was a young child. They had returned from an evening out, had crept in to see her and she was waking blearily from sleep, focusing slowly on the two figures lit by a shaft of light through the open door. They were smiling and, in the sleepy, soap-scented warmth of her bed, the smell of her father's breath was strange but comforting as he bent down to kiss her goodnight.

Julie gasped aloud.

No. It couldn't be. She must have made a mistake.

She closed her eyes, squeezed the eyelids down hard, then opened them again to stare into the dark. Had Sarah realised? Was that what she had meant?

It was no mistake. Her father ten years ago; the man in the photograph. There was little difference.

For a long time Julie lay with her eyes opened.

She woke without knowing why.

The room swam blackly around her; it must only be the early hours of the morning. For a moment she lay on her side, considering whether to close her eyes and go back to sleep, or to roll over and check the time. She turned lazily half-way and lay on her back. Then she noticed. Something about the room was different. It was not dark enough. At the bottom of the bed something happened to it. Between the hard edges of the wall and door there was a wedge of greyness that told her the door was open. Why? She hadn't left it open and it couldn't have sprung open by itself. It was not until she turned fully to face the room, however, that she realised she was not alone.

Someone was sitting on the chair by the dressing table, sitting very still and watching her in the dark.

She sat quickly upright.

"Dad? Is that you?"

The answer was a rasping whisper from the darkness. "I'm sorry, Julie. I wanted to wake you but I wasn't sure how. I didn't want to shock you."

"Shock me?" She tried to see his face but he remained a blurred outline. She reached towards the bedside lamp, feeling her way along the flex until her hands met the tiny click-switch. The sudden brightness made her squint. The dial on the watchface showed two fifty-three.

"I mean, by waking you up too quickly. That's why I waited."

She was awake by now but still it was difficult to see him properly, sitting as he was beyond the light from the lamp. It disconcerted her. She pushed a pillow upright behind her and propped herself against it. "Come and sit here," she said. "I can't see you properly."

Almost in slow motion he moved to the side of the bed and sat, level with her knees. Then he said, "Julie. What would you say if I told you I was thinking of divorce?"

"If you did what?"

"Yes. If your mother and I were to get a divorce?"

Julie shook her head in confusion. "Why are you asking me now?"

"Because it's important. Please. Tell me what you think."

"At three o'clock in the morning?"

"Yes, at three o'clock in the morning." The words came out as a whine, the appeal of a small child determined to get its own way. "Please, Julie. It's been preying on my mind. I couldn't sleep."

"I don't believe this."

"Just tell me," he insisted.

"OK. All right. Do I reckon you should get a divorce? Yes, if you want to."

He had been waiting for something more: an invitation to talk, not an abrupt dismissal. He stumbled over his words. "You really . . . I mean, it would be . . . it would be a big step wouldn't it?"

"Dad, look. I don't know what you should do. Don't try and get me to make the decision for you, because that isn't fair."

He sounded hurt. "I wasn't . . . I didn't mean it to sound like that. I just wanted to talk it through with someone."

"How about Mum. Have you talked it through with her?"

"No," he sighed. "She's not been in the mood for listening recently. Hadn't you noticed?"

"I'm sorry." She reached out to take his hand then stopped, drew back and rested it on the covers close to his, but not touching. "Of course we have to talk about it," she said. "But do we have to do it now? I'm ever so tired, Dad. It's very hard to think straight."

He patted the back of her hand and she tensed perceptibly.

"What's the matter?" he asked. "You seem . . . I don't know — uneasy."

"Just tired."

"Alright, I'll let you get some sleep. Sorry." Reluctantly he stood up and walked partway to the door.

"Goodnight," she said and reached over to put out the light.

"No. Wait a minute."

Before she realised what was happening, he had rushed to the bedside table and held her wrist tightly.

"Dad!" The pressure hurt and he had begun to frighten her. "Please let go."

Immediately he loosed his grip. Julie was horrified to see his hand shaking.

"What is it?" she demanded.

He shook his head mutely.

"What's going on? What's happened?"

When at last he spoke, Julie could not tell if it was to her or only for himself. The words had no tone or expression.

"I went in to see how she was," he said. "About eleven, after you'd come to bed. She was sleeping. She looked quite calm: all the strain had gone from her face. And I thought it would all be so easy."

Julie felt the muscles in her chest contract. Involuntarily she began to hold her breath and her heart pulsed frantically.

"I closed the door," he intoned, "and went to bed. But I couldn't sleep. I kept trying to work out the best way to do it. The least painful — for everyone. The more I thought about it, the more I felt I was doing it for her. In the end I went to the bathroom, to the cabinet where her pills are. I counted them out. There were twenty of them."

Stop! Julie screamed in her head but his voice poured out relentlessly, drowning her words before she could form them.

"I lay them out in a line along the edge of the bath. I thought about how to get her to take them: a few at a time or all together. Julie." He was looking at her now but his eyes were blank. "I felt the bottle in my hand. It was cold and hard, and suddenly my hands began to shake. I put all the pills back, one at a time, and then the bottle. Then I came in here to wake you up."

Julie's heart lurched back to life. For a second she was gasping for air. "You didn't . . . do anything?" she said.

"No," he whispered. "I didn't do anything."

As if he was a cleverly articulated puppet whose strings had been snapped, he knelt suddenly on the floor and put his arms clumsily round Julie, pressing his head into the crook of her neck. He began to cry and every word was like a small scream wrung from his heaving chest.

"I didn't . . . Oh, Julie, but I wanted to. I had to tell you. To make sure it never happened. I had to."

She tried to comfort him but it was no use: her arm rested heavily on his shoulder and the longer she felt the weight of his physical presence against her, the more she felt herself flinch and draw away inside, until at last it became unbearable and she pulled away, pressing herself against the wall.

He sat slumped and immobile on the edge of the bed.

"Just give me a minute and I'll be all right," he said.

Within the minute he had gone, the door clicking softly shut behind him.

However hard she tried, Julie could not get warm again. She curled up and pulled the bedclothes tight over her shoulders and neck, but she knew she would not sleep. Dragging the blanket around her like an outsized cloak, she leaned against the wall and planned what to do.

How could he, she thought angrily, how could he even think of doing that? And then coming to tell me as if I'm some sort of priest he can confess his sins to. She would not absolve him, though. She had tried to feel sympathy for him but found none in her.

And suddenly she knew what she had to do.

It took her a couple of minutes to get dressed. She put on jeans and the warmest jumper she could find, then packed a few odds and ends into her overnight bag and left the room. There was a light switch on the wall close by but she ignored it, moving cautiously down the darkened landing to the bathroom. The tap on the washbasin was dripping. She methodically turned it off before picking up her toothbrush and dropping it into the bag.

Having manoeuvred the staircase, she felt for her duffel coat on the pegs in the hall, checked that her gloves were still in the pocket and stepped out into the frosty night.

Sarah's house was about a mile away. Julie wondered if her parents would, after all, object. Sarah probably hadn't thought to mention it to them yet and they would hardly be too pleased at being woken at four in the morning, especially to have their house used as a hotel. She imagined herself standing on the doorstep; hearing the doorbell echo through the sleeping house; seeing a light go on in an upstairs room, a face peering irritably from the lighted window: waiting for the footsteps at the bottom of the stairs and at long last the door opening. They would have no idea what she was doing there. She would have to stand there shivering and explain all that had happened.

Two streets away she stopped. No. She couldn't go through with that, not yet at any rate. She needed more time to think. There was a small park on the hill leading down to the station where she sometimes went to be alone. It was only half a mile away. There would be a bench to sit on and no-one at this improbable hour to disturb her.

It took her fifteen minutes to get there.

She entered the park through a small iron gate rusted dark brown with age. Beyond it a metalled footpath curved towards a footbridge in the distance: one side the hard rutted grass of a football pitch, and on the other the steep embankment sloping down to the railway track. A spiked fence denoted the border, against which hundreds of large brown leaves had been scooped, dry and brittle-frosty.

Halfway along, the path was elevated enough for Julie to look down into the siding and goods yard beneath. Gantries of skeletal grey steel stretched into the distance, overlapping in her view to form one huge metal grid. The top of the nearest gantry was just beyond the fence, level with Julie's feet and sporting its own protective barrier of spikes. She walked on, up to the bridge.

During her journey from the house she had become less aware of the freezing cold; it took little time, once she was standing still, for the cold to reclaim her. Despite the hood on her duffel coat, her nose and cheeks began to hurt. She pushed it back off her head, shook loose her hair and gulped in the bitter cold. It was exhilarating.

The parapet was high but, by stretching up her arms as far as possible, she was able to grip the ledge and pull herself up so her face was level with the top. You would, she decided, have to be a very agile and desperate suicide: even here vicious spikes were set into the top at the far edge, angled inwards for maximum effect. You'd be far more likely to slip and land on the spikes, and somehow that wouldn't be doing the thing properly.

Did her mother think things out like this before reaching for the pills or switching on the unlit gas fire? Did she calculate how close she could get to dying without actually succeeding? Maybe that's why she'd never tried to jump. A girl at school had been walking past the multi-storey car park in town, when a man had thrown himself off the top. There was no way of bringing him back to life. A sixty-foot jump was inexorable.

Mrs Ashcroft always gave people a chance. She must have known, when she turned on the gas, that Julie or her father would be home in time. With her it was far more complicated, a game whose rules were set down in advance. Anyone not involved would have said it added up to a cry for help.

So why, when they tried to help, did she constantly and steadfastly refuse it? Had she built such a wall around her that she could not reach out even if she wanted to? Questions. That's all there ever were. Questions and more questions; and instead of answers, all Julie could see were recurring images of death. But maybe even here there was an answer of sorts. For wasn't Mrs Ashcroft really a woman drowning, thrashing out at those who tried to save her, fighting and dragging them under; anything rather than let herself be pulled to safety?

Well, kick and struggle as they might, you didn't *let* someone drown, did you? You didn't stand at the side and say, "Go on then. Drown yourself if that's really what you want to do." Because you knew they didn't, any more than her mother really wanted to die. What she wanted was proof that life was worth something, that her own life was worthwhile to others. And if Julie and her father didn't produce the evidence, then they were helping to kill her. There was no such thing as hopelessness, only helplessness.

The lights along the gantries picked out the silver rails, gliding towards each other and merging in the distance.

Julie set off for home.

Mr Gostelow's Demon

Mr Gostelow locked the church at six o'clock on winter evenings. It was a routine that had not varied for twenty-three years: the bolting of the door at the West End; the methodical extinguishing of lights in the nave and chancel. His tall, striding figure seemed by now a part of the furnishings.

As he paced the ancient flagstones of the south aisle, his stout shoes creaked and the folds of his black cassock rustled drily. On the leaded roof the sound echoed back as a flock of starlings suddenly took flight.

Mr Gostelow paused by a light switch at the side of the chancel arch and, with the ceasing of his footsteps, silence resumed its hold upon the church. The building stood alone, surrounded by fields: a tall-masted ship in a sea of furrows. At most times the only noise was the wind.

The church had been built at a time of great prosperity. Its stone vaults were higher than any church for miles around. Its windows had once held magnificent glass: dark blue and bright crimson. Most of that had gone, pounded to dust by the boots and hammers of the reformers. But the church's finest glory had survived. Painted over, later uncovered and now expertly restored, the *Last Judgement* filled the lofty chancel arch.

It was a fearsome masterpiece. At its base, the souls of the dead rose naked from their graves; above them, in splendid armour, the Archangel Michael weighed their sins in the balance; and over all the giant figure of God sat watching, enthroned on a blazing rainbow. On his right the blessed ascended the stairway to Heaven, while on his left cowered the souls of the Damned. Tortured by grotesque demons, they were thrust, beaten and shovelled into the waiting jaws of an obscene monster, its teeth like sharpened slivers of glass. For centuries this terrifying vision had served to show worshippers the price of their sins.

Mr Gostelow, however, did not even glance up as he pressed the switch that plunged it into darkness. He had never understood why it attracted the attention of so many visitors and scholars. It was, after all, merely a product of its age: an age of superstition and ignorance. As such, it had nothing to do with him.

He was a devout man, certainly, but unafflicted by the curse of imagination. Though sixty-seven years old, body and morals remained as one: unerringly upright. Throughout every service he would sit in his oak stall behind the vicar, his head visible from the back of the church, his verger's staff like a flagpole at his side. Were he bearded, it would not have been difficult to imagine him as one of those stern Old Testament prophets, or even, when his sharp eye glared down at a fidgeting choirboy freezing him to inert obedience, with the great judge Himself.

Mr Gostelow continued on his round. When he reached the vestry door, he opened it and pressed a switch inside before shutting off the light over the altar. A finger of pale yellow reached out from the doorway and slanted across the aisle, picking out the carved figures on a nearby monument. He stepped into the carpeted comfort of the vestry and closed the door, then from a large cupboard in the corner he withdrew his warm winter coat, replaced his cassock on its hanger and left.

The outside door was on a safety lock. Having slammed it hard, he picked his way round sagging rows of headstones until he reached the rusty iron gate. It would take him eight minutes on the footpath to reach his cottage. It was a dark journey and he had to be nimble on his feet in places, but he knew it as well as he knew himself. And it was a full seven minutes shorter than the winding road into the village. Head down against the cold wind, he tacked down the edge of the fields and over stiles.

The churchyard of St Michael and All Angels was a desolate place at the best of times. Those buried in its now frozen ground might well be waiting 'in sure and certain hope of the life to come' but, on the evidence of the surroundings, only a confirmed optimist would have placed bets on its happening. The few trees around its edge had been savaged by centuries of wind and gnawing cold, and only the most tenacious remained. Even the short, hardy yew trees, standing sentinel on the path to the North door, bowed their heads with an air of imminent defeat.

Yet, because these trees were surrounded by acres of open countryside with not a copse or thicket in sight, they had become the bearers of many hearts and weather-stained initials carved by the village lovers. One in particular, a single ancient oak which stood at the furthest corner of the cemetery, had been witness to many scenes of affection, even recently — as recently, in fact, as the previous Sunday. But on that occasion there had been another, unseen, witness.

It was not until the following day that Mr Gostelow acted upon what he had seen, but when he did, it was with a resoluteness appropriate to his distasteful task. No doubt the eye of God had been watching too but it fell to Mr Gostelow to make the phone call from the telephone box in the village. He waited patiently, his breath steaming the small panes of glass, until the ringing tone abruptly stopped.

"Hello," a brisk voice at the other end cracked. "Stainsforth 7962."

"Hello. Colonel Mostyn?"

"Yes. Speaking."

"This is Ernest Gostelow, from St Michael's."

"Gostelow. Yes, what can I do for you?"

Mr Gostelow cleared his throat, an action intended as a comment in itself. "It is a little delicate," he said. "The matter I wish to talk to you about. Perhaps I might come and see you to explain."

There was a distinct pause before the Colonel's puzzled voice replied, "I don't quite see . . ."

"It concerns your son, Colonel. Your youngest son."

"Really? Well, in that case, you'd better come up to the house, I suppose. Shall we say this afternoon some time? Say, half past four?"

"Certainly," Mr Gostelow agreed. "Thank you. Goodbye."

It was a spacious house, comfortable but not quite a mansion. An enterprising Edwardian businessman, a manufacturer of wrought-iron brackets and other decorative fittings, had had it built in the style of the times. It had low, sweeping gables, now covered with ivy that framed the stone-mullioned windows; steep-pitched roofs streamlined it against the prevailing winds, and its modest landscaped garden made a brave attempt to mitigate the bleakness of the surrounding flatlands.

Colonel Mostyn had lived there since his parents had acquired the house, nearly fifty years before, and by now the building and the family that lived in it were a firm part of local life. His two eldest boys had both left home, one to join the Air Force and the other to begin a promising career in the City; his daughter was at university, not at Oxford or Cambridge as he would ideally have wished, but at a sound London college nonetheless. That left the Colonel, his wife Adele and Paul; and with only the three of them in such a spacious house, Paul enjoyed a considerable amount of independence. He was eleven.

Paul's bedroom was situated in the gable end facing the drive. From here he could see everything that happened below and identify all visitors long before they reached the front door. When Derek and Stephen had been living at home, his inquisitiveness had been well rewarded with troupes of their acquaintances and girlfriends. Sandra, too, could be relied upon to produce some interesting company. But nowadays things were decidedly dull. Tedious and predictable.

He was just reflecting on the unchanging landscape at the front of the house, when he noticed the figure walking. At first, all he could see was a head and shoulders moving along the line of the wall by the road. Paul moved closer to the window and squinted up the drive in an attempt to identify this unaccustomed visitor.

The man was tall, but it was difficult to tell how old he was from his walk; an old forty-five or a young seventy. Paul frowned in concentration. Only when the figure was two-thirds of the way down the drive, did he suddenly realise that Mr Gostelow, the church warden, was paying them a visit.

The Colonel himself answered the door and ushered Mr Gostelow into the main drawing room. The church warden cast a stern eye over its contents: large sofa, two round wooden tables, one supporting a copy of *Country Life*, polished parquet floor and a large Persian rug.

The Colonel indicated the vacant sofa. "Would you care to sit down, Mr Gostelow?"

Bowing slightly by way of answer, Mr Gostelow took up a position near the edge of the sofa, carefully avoiding the comfortable cushions lying in wait behind. "Colonel Mostyn," he began. "I don't quite know how to tell you this . . ." His face creased in convincing uncertainty.

"Well," the Colonel prompted. "I'm sure you haven't come to see me — made an appointment even — to tell me you don't know what to say." He found this sort of bluff humour usually put people at their ease, but on this occasion it seemed, if anything, to make the old man perched on his sofa even more uncomfortable. He said nothing, and his silence grew menacing with each passing second.

Finally he said, "I fear your son is tainted by homosexuality."

Colonel Mostyn had been standing with his hands in his pockets, waiting patiently for this aggravating old man to say his piece and go. Now, he stayed momentarily quite still, as if nothing had been said at all. His mouth opened to speak but no words came. He scowled, shook his head and abruptly laughed.

"This is preposterous," he said.

"I'm afraid there can be little doubt, Colonel Mostyn. I saw it with my own eyes."

"Saw what?" The Colonel hovered between anger and anxiety.

Mr Gostelow began his carefully rehearsed recital. "Your son, being a choirboy at St Michael's, is quite well known to me," he said. "I see him regularly, not to speak to, but I know him well enough by sight not to mistake his face for that of another boy."

"Go on," the Colonel rasped.

"What I mean to say is that I could not have been mistaken. It was your son I saw with one of the senior choristers: a boy named Martin Truett. I noticed them first when they were getting changed after the service. They were taking more time over it than they needed, as if they were trying to be the last to leave. I wondered why. Some boys I would have suspected of planning some sort of vandalism, but I didn't think that was likely with your son. At any rate, I watched them closely and, sure enough, they were the last of the boys to go. It was from the window in the vestry that I saw what happened."

Mr Gostelow removed a large handkerchief from his jacket pocket and wiped his mouth, as if to rid it of an unpleasant taste. "They walked off in the direction of the lych-gate," he continued determinedly, "but when they were about halfway there, the older boy — Truett — stopped. He looked around him, presumably to make sure no-one was watching, then the two of them turned and walked slowly to the corner of the churchyard. They were standing very close to each other; they were laughing, I think. Then the Truett boy moved right up to the tree. For a moment I lost sight of him and the next I saw was the two of them, holding each other and — kissing."

The Colonel appeared to be studying the pattern of the rug on which he stood, his feet planted firmly far enough apart to preserve some sense of balance. "You are," he said slowly, raising his eyes to meet those of the church warden, "absolutely sure of this?" The fists which hung clenched at his side intimated what he might do should the story prove false.

"There can be no doubt," said Mr Gostelow.

Without waiting to be shown out, he left the Colonel standing in the drawing room and returned to the hallway. From between the banisters of the upper landing, where he had rapidly retreated, Paul watched the old man open the front door and leave. His heavy footsteps boomed back along the drive.

"I know he's a pompous, interfering old man, but that doesn't alter what he saw." Some of the abruptness in Colonel Mostyn's voice was dissipated by the layers of leather-bound books that walled the study, but his wife, Adele, knew she must tread cautiously. She was only too aware of her husband's impetuosity and flights of temper; she had been married to them for twenty-six years. She could also tell when he was genuinely worried.

"Darling, it wouldn't be the first time two boys had been involved in a . . . friendship of this sort. You must surely have known boys when you were at school who walked around arm in arm, or had crushes on older boys. It happens all the time at that age."

"Maybe so, Adele, but not to the point of kissing in public." The Colonel regarded his wife sceptically. "I must say, you seem to be taking it all very calmly," he said. "Anything could have been going on behind our backs; anything at all."

He broke off and shook his head, as if to clear it of the uncomfortable thoughts provoked by his remark.

Mrs Mostyn had been sitting patiently in the window seat. Seeing her husband floundering helplessly in front of her, she leaned forward, stretched out her hand and drew him into the space beside her.

"Really," she said gently, "I'm sure there's very little to worry about. Under normal circumstances, I'd suggest we leave it alone altogether. It's a passing phase; it'll probably all be over and forgotten by next summer."

Her husband frowned. "You said 'under normal circumstances'."

She pursed her lips in thought. "That's right," she said. "But now that Mr Gostelow has made his presence felt . . . He must have eyes like a hawk. I mean, the corner of the graveyard doesn't normally qualify as a public place, does it? Perhaps we *should* have a tactful word with Paul. I think it might be best if I dealt with it by myself, to start with, at least."

Colonel Mostyn made to object, changed his mind and kissed his wife gratefully on the cheek. "Yes," he said, "you're right. I'm sure you're right."

From the lightness of the knock on his bedroom door, Paul knew that his moment of horror had been delayed a little longer. For a quarter of an hour since the old man had left, he had been waiting for his father; ever since he had tiptoed downstairs, pressed his ear to the rough grain of the drawing room door, wanting to hear more clearly — not wanting to hear. Shakily, he had turned back up the stairs.

And now this gentle, almost timid knocking.

"Yes," he answered, and his voice was swallowed by the room.

His mother came in, closed the door and stood looking at the solitary figure of her son.

Sitting quickly and clumsily on the bed at his side, she held him close. He remained rigid as ice in her arms. Then in a moment he was crying, and the dampness of his tears against her bare arm consoled her. For fully five minutes they remained together, motionless but for the sporadic rocking — backwards, forwards — when his sobbing grew more fierce.

At length he stopped. "Here," she said, and reached beneath the pillow for the clean handkerchief she knew would be there. She gave it to him and he snuffled into it, pausing only to wipe his eyes. Relieved, yet ashamed, he rubbed hard at the salt-swollen flesh. His mother reached out and held his wrist. "Do you want to talk about it?" she said.

How could anyone reconstruct the past, moment by moment? For that was what he must do in order to explain: stand outside himself, detached; an observer of every action, recorder of each word exchanged between the two of them in that quiet and seemingly private churchyard the day before . . . .

"It won't do, you know," Martin said, shaking his head in mock seriousness. "Honestly, I'm not such a splendid person as you seem to think I am."

"I know what you're going to say."

The older boy stopped and smiled at Paul. "Are you a mind-reader or something?"

"No," Paul continued in the same tone of despondency. "But I still know. You're going to tell me that I've got a crush on you; that it's not love, I only *think* it is and that I'll grow out of soon."

Martin laughed, then caught sight of Paul's defiant face and stopped. "You're right," he conceded. "That's exactly what I was going to say."

"Well, you're wrong."

Martin nodded towards the tree in the far corner of the graveyard. "See that big tree over there?"

"Are you changing the subject?" Paul scowled indignantly.

"No. Let's walk over there for a minute." He checked cautiously around him in case any of the other boys had lingered by the gate. "I just want to point something out to you."

"Alright," Paul shrugged. He was in no hurry. So long as it meant he could spend a little more time with Martin.

They walked steadily across the churchyard, off the path and across the grass between the tipsy gravestones. Beneath the large oak the ground was bare: dark, damp earth where neither grass nor weeds grew. Overhead, the branches dipped and lifted, their tops scraping the sky.

"Here," said Martin. "See these?"

He pointed to two pairs of initials at about chest height. Paul leaned forward to see: "M.T." he read aloud, and turned to see Martin grinning rather sheepishly at his side. "Is that you? It is, isn't it?"

Martin nodded.

"Why have you gone all quiet?"

Both boys were grinning now and suddenly the laughter, dammed up inside, burst out. When it subsided enough to speak again, Paul asked, "Were you embarrassed?"

"A bit, I suppose."

"Whose are the other initials then?"

"Someone who was my hero for nearly a year: a boy in the sixth form at school when I was in the first year. It took me months to pluck up the courage to speak to him. He was very pleasant. After a while he even did things like helping with my Maths homework during Breaktime. He never made out I was a nuisance, so I think he liked me too. But of course I thought he was wonderful. I used to imagine how we'd become really good friends and go places together, and I didn't really care what it was we'd *do*; all that mattered was that I'd be with him. When he left school I was very upset. That was when I came and carved this."

"And what happened after that?" Paul asked, intrigued.

"Nothing."

"Didn't you even see him again?"

"No. He didn't come back home often and when he did, he was too busy with his own friends, I suppose. Anyhow, I don't know quite what happened, but I suddenly realised I'd stopped missing him; I was just being moody for something to do. Maybe I'd even started to enjoy it, I don't know. Now I can't remember what he looked like properly."

Paul scuffed the earth beneath his feet. "What you

mean," he said dejectedly, "is that you reckon it'll be the same with me."

"Yes."

"Oh." Paul stared at the ground and sighed.

Martin put a hand gently on his shoulder. "I don't know, I just think it might be, that's all." As he took his hand away he saw the look of despair on the younger boy's face. "I'm sorry."

Paul shrugged carelessly. "It's OK," he said, and then a mischievous look sparkled to the surface. "I'll stop pestering you, on one condition."

"All right," Martin smiled. "Name your price."

Paul edged closer and stared into his eyes. "A kiss."

The smile wavered. Martin could see that he meant it. "Just one."

Martin thought hard before replying. "On one condition," he said. "I can make conditions too; that's only fair."

"What?"

"That you understand what it means. It's a sign of friendship. An end to thinking of love, not a beginning."

Paul cocked his head to one side and pretended to debate the matter. "All right," he said chirpily. "Agreed."

And so, for one second, they had kissed. It was probably the shortest embrace ever shared beneath that tree, in its secluded corner of the graveyard.

An end, not a beginning.

And so, in a way, it was.

Justice has two tasks to perform: the protection of the weak and the punishment of the guilty.

This was the thought uppermost in Mr Gostelow's mind as he made the return journey to his cottage. The early evening was damp with a hint of ground-mist rising in the hollows of surrounding fields. Despite his overcoat and muffler, Mr Gostelow's bones ached. The early, damp days of winter were always the worst, far more debilitating than the later ice and snow. He longed for the crisp, fresh air to come.

It was a relief to be home, to shut out the weather behind a stout wooden door and heavy curtains. The thought was shut out less easily. Try as he might, he could not rid himself of that scene in the churchyard, and each new contemplation of it served merely to fan the flames of his righteous anger. The younger boy was inexperienced, impressionable. For him there might be some mitigation. But the older one—no; he must be shown for what he was.

Martin Truett was thirteen and a half, and remarkably talented. Everyone was agreed on that. Unfortunately, his aptitude was in a field considered quite irrelevant by his father, a heavily-built man who worked as manager of a small hardware shop in the nearest town. He had long entertained aspirations for his son in the legal profession. Not that he liked solicitors: most of them were greasy little men whose patronising behaviour aggravated him considerably. But even he had been quick to notice that their success brought them wealth. Never having possessed money in any quantity himself, he felt it his duty to thrust his son firmly in the direction of any that might be going begging. This ambition he pursued all the more fervently because he had just the one chance to achieve it: Martin was an only child.

During the last few months encounters between father and son had become increasingly frequent and hostile. The most common battle-ground was the dinner or breakfast table; and the issue in dispute was the area on which they had the strongest, most divided opinions: Martin's future career. For Martin was as adamant as his father in which direction his future lay. He was going to perform, and with luck compose, music.

The time was fast approaching when he must select subjects for 'O' level study, and Music was in the same block of options as R.E., Needlework and Chemistry. Every time the matter was discussed, his father would insist that as Chemistry was the only 'useful' subject on the list, that was what he must do. Martin would point out that Needlework would be just as useful to a prospective lawyer; Mr Truett would warn him to watch how he spoke to his father and then made his final pronouncement on the subject: if he had wanted his son to study Music, he would have sent him to a girls' school.

At that point events would rapidly soar out of control: Martin shouting, his father yelling back and Mrs Truett watching but saying nothing; until finally Mr Truett would push back his chair, walk purposefully round the table, and hit his son around the head with a fist shaped by twenty-five years of manual work. Only after he had stormed out of the room did Mrs Truett dare to comfort her son.

For his part, each unfair pummelling at the hands of his father made Martin more determined. It was this determination, with some support from his mother, that had kept him his place in the choir. And so far, though his father was scornful of the time spent in church, he had not expressly forbidden it. He was unaware of the piano lessons his son also received during school time, and both Martin and his mother lived in dread of the day he found out.

Today, dinner had been a darkly brooding affair, rather than the raging tempest to which they had grown accustomed. The main reason was his father's headache. He had not admitted to having one, of course; he never did. But Martin and his mother could tell by the way he scowled at his place and took his second cup of tea down to the shed where he was working on repairing his bike. In his absence it actually seemed possible to look forward to an evening of peace and relaxation.

The Truett's house was at the far end of the village. It was a small semi-detached council dwelling, set in a crescent of identical buildings clustered around a small green. A narrow road separated it from the private houses that constituted the last part of the 'real' village in most people's eyes.

The backs of the houses on one side of the crescent looked directly on to open fields, while those on the Truett's side abutted the village allotments. Beyond these was a patch of scrubby, open ground which the council had for years threatened to build on. And a little way beyond that lay the expanse of Stainsforth Reservoir, a cheerless stretch of water that did nothing to soften the surrounding landscape, merely substituting its own grey flatness for the furrowed brown flatness of the fields.

As Mr Gostelow headed determinedly up the shabby road, its neglected fences and hedgerows filled him with depression. In the damp silence his breath mingled with the now heavy mist around him. He had no desire to be here in this alien wilderness of pebbledash house fronts and overgrown gardens. And Mr Truett carried with him the reputation of a violent man. For a moment Mr Gostelow experienced a powerful urge to abandon his mission, to turn and hurry back to the comfortable warmth of his own cottage. But duty pushed him forward.

At the edge of the green he stopped once more to check the first house number. He glanced round the semicircle, ticking off the numbers as he went. So, the Truett's house was that one over on the right, the one with the brown front door and a single light on in the living room.

Mr Gostelow cut diagonally over the green, crossed the road and pushed open the low, wooden gate.

Stumbling, crashing through the allotments beyond the back garden, Martin felt his head burst with pain and confusion. For years he had known his father believed his fists to be an acceptable substitute for argument, but never — never in his whole life — had he used them like that before: on and on, each blow a prelude to the next. Harder and harder.

His mother had done her best, pleading with her husband, trying to hold him back. She had been thrust away and stood helplessly, her tear-stained face to the wall, while behind her the savage attack continued unchecked.

As for Martin, he had quickly realised that any attempt at resistance was quite useless. He could only cover his head with his arms and try to protect himself that way. It was bizarre that, in the middle of this hurricane, buffetted whichever way he turned, a part of his mind remained clear and unaffected: a sort of automatic pilot that clinically charted each move. Only when he had been forced to the floor did it give out on him completely, and he dropped his guard to cling to the arm of the sofa. He registered one last picture, of his mother's sobbing back, the figure of his father towering lop-sidedly over him, and then a rock had crashed into his head, between the top of his cheekbone and his left temple, thrusting him through a crimson curtain of pain into momentary unconsciousness.

He had re-emerged to see his parents struggling in the middle of the room, his mother shaking her head and screaming while Mr Truett held her by the shoulders, fighting to control his own anger and his wife's hysteria. Dazedly, Martin had stood and walked past them into the kitchen, grabbing the door frame for support, then out of the back door. Blinking hard, he had put one foot experimentally in front of the other, discovered he could move without falling, and shambled into a loping run towards the gate at the bottom of the garden. Before his father appeared at the back door, he was out into the entry and through a gap in the allotment hedge.

But what was the point in his running? He couldn't stay out here for ever. Already the damp chill of the night air was seeping through his jumper, making him shiver violently each time he stopped to draw breath. He shook his head, trying to clear his bruised thoughts. How could he ever go back to face again that anger and disgust; to fight the abuse and knotted fists? No. It was impossible. He blundered onwards past the allotments and into the open scrubland beyond, mist swimming thickly around him.

Before he realised where he had been heading, he was standing at the edge of the reservoir looking down into the grey water, that spread out before him like an undiscovered country in the hovering mist.

A week of falling temperatures and the advent of frost separated Mr Gostelow from the events of that Monday night. In other respects, too, it had been a bitter time but, as he approached the back garden of his cottage by the field path, Mr Gostelow refused to think any more about it. It was, after all, no longer his concern.

He let himself in through the back door into the kitchen and soon had a kettle steaming away on the hob, in preparation for a warming winter nightcap.

By ten o'clock he was in bed and sleeping the sleep of the righteous.

The following day was a Saturday. Mr Gostelow was in the church early, tidying and arranging: there would be visitors arriving and guidebooks to sell. It was a dull morning so he switched on the lights.

He had just unlocked the cupboard containing postcards of the church, when he stopped suddenly and listened. His ears were attuned to all the usual background distractions; he could even distinguish the quiet swinging of the ropes in the bell tower. But, just for a moment, there had been something else: an odd scurrying sound from the other end of the church. It had happened before that a stray cat had wandered in out of curiosity, but Mr Gostelow remembered no doors left open today. He rose and placed the cards next to the appropriate moneybox. Perhaps he should investigate.

Then he heard voices and the crunch of gravel on the path outside. Next moment a small party of visitors, cameras slung over their shoulders, stepped eagerly into the church. Mr Gostelow turned to greet them.

"Welcome to St Michael's" he said. "I should like to point out before you commence your visit, that photography inside the church is not permitted." He indicated a notice to their left. The group immediately assumed a respectful quiet, whether in awe at the majestic building or in deference to the church warden it was difficult to say.

"I shall be available in the vestry if you require any assistance," he continued. With a slight nod of the head he turned and walked away.

As he approached the further end of the church, he remembered the noise. He walked round behind the choirscreen and stepped into the row of carved pews reserved for the clergy. He held on to the sloped wooden ledge on which centuries of psalters and hymn books had been rested, rubbing the grain to a glassy smoothness, and bent over to look beneath the seats. A carved bench end, shaped like a man's head and sprouting leaves from its distorted mouth, leered up at him, but of the noise-maker there was nothing to be seen.

Straightening up again, he crossed the chancel and repeated the procedure on the other side. Again nothing. But he *had* heard a noise, and he was not in the habit of imagining things. He stood very still at the edge of the choirstalls and thought. In this attitude of frozen concentration he might almost have been taken for an elaborate life-size carving; the masterpiece of some enterprising mediaeval artisan. At last he stepped down to the floor of the chancel and strode up to the polished brass rail that separated the choir from the sanctuary beyond. Unclipping the rope in the middle he approached the altar.

Hoping that no-one was watching, he lifted the skirts of the altar cloth to peer beneath. It was dark there and smelled of dust. He dropped the covering and it swished heavily back into place.

Again he paused, listening now for the sound that eluded him. Further off, the group of tourists babbled quietly. The vast building picked up the sound, tossing it roughly against pillars, dragging it along aisles and transepts, and finally lifting it upwards till it disappeared into the hollow vaults. Against those pervasive noises it was impossible for Mr Gostelow to discern anything clearly. Mildly annoyed, he replaced the altar rope and set off for the vestry.

"Excuse me," a voice called shrilly.

Mr Gostelow turned to see a middle-aged lady in a tweed suit bearing down upon him. What did she want? Frequently he was expected to give a tour of the building, a service he had no intention of providing. What did they think the guidebook was for?

"I wonder if you'd be kind enough to explain something," she demanded, turned tail and headed back the way she had come. Clearly she expected him to follow. She stopped by the chancel arch and pointed upwards. "Why has the painting been altered?" she asked.

Mr Gostelow frowned. Whatever questions he might have anticipated, this was certainly not one of them.

"The painting," she repeated. "If you look at the photograph in the book, you'll see what I mean."

She handed it to him, and he glanced from photograph

to painting and back again. "I'm afraid I don't see . . ."

"Look," she insisted. "Over on that side. In the photograph there's a devil thing with horns, but he's not there in the painting."

Mr Gostelow craned his neck backwards and examined the wall more closely. Had the floodlight not been on, he would have attributed what he saw to an optical illusion; an effect of shadows and light caused by the building itself. But there could be no doubt: one of the demons in the Hell scene was no longer there.

Why on earth had it been painted out and, more to the point, who had done it without his knowledge? The vicar perhaps? It was possible. He was a most unpredictable sort of man and there was no love lost between them. But for what reason? He, unlike Mr Gostelow, was a great admirer of this savage picture — this 'awesome vision' as he enthusiastically referred to it. In which case some other person must have entered the church, without his knowledge . . .

"Ah, yes!" he said aloud. "I believe it has something to do with protecting that area from damp. A protective covering; yes. I'm sure it will be removed again soon."

"Oh, I see," the woman beamed. "Thank you for your help."

In due time the party left. No more questions had been asked and the coffers were fuller than before. But the more he thought about the missing figure, the more annoyed Mr Gostelow had become. He had no great affection for the picture, certainly, but an act of such deliberate vandalism, and in *his* church, was not to be taken lightly.

As the voices receded down the path, he dragged the

tall stepladder from its niche in an obscure corner of the North transept and into the body of the empty church. It scraped noisily on the stone floor. Propping it against the pillar to the right of the chancel arch, he steadied it before climbing carefully upwards. Twelve rungs up he stopped, his head level with the monster representing Hell. Just above and to the left was where the missing figure should have been.

Mr Gostelow stared at the empty space. Surely not?

Holding on to the pillar for extra support, he leaned sideways as far as he dared and stretched out his arm to touch the wall. His finger met bare stonework. There was no paint there.

Mr Gostelow was appalled. There was no way of repairing this sort of damage; it was permanent. He ran his hand again round the damaged area and noted how cleanly and precisely it had been done. Not a single figure around it had been touched. He was so absorbed in thought that he failed to hear the footsteps approaching him from below.

"Mr Gostelow."

The voice startled him. His foot slipped on the rounded rung of the ladder and he grabbed quickly for the pillar, grazing his hand. Mr Dalziel, the vicar, waited patiently at the base of the steps. "Could I have a word with you, please?" he asked.

Mr Gostelow was scowling as he reached the ground. "That was, if I may say so, a very irresponsible thing to do, Vicar. I might easily have come to grief." He rubbed his wounded hand ruefully. "You completely startled me."

Mr Dalziel took a deep breath. "I'm sorry," he said. "It was not intentional."

Mr Gostelow gave him what he hoped was a clear look of steely reprimand and waited to discover why he was required. Always, when the two men had cause to speak, it was the vicar who found himself slipping into tones of deference and respect.

Now, suppressed anger made him all the more uncertain what words to choose. "Perhaps," he managed at last, "we could speak in the vestry." They walked there in silence.

Mr Dalziel waited until the door was firmly closed before he began. "As you are aware, Mr Gostelow," he said, "the services in this parish are held on a rotary basis and we were not due to use St Michael's again for another week. However, owing to problems with the heating at St Giles', it has been decided to hold evensong here today."

Mr Gostelow raised an eyebrow and tutted gently. "I must say, Vicar, this is rather short notice."

"I realise," Mr Dalziel continued, "that there may be some slight inconvenience, but I'm sure you're more than capable of making the necessary arrangements. It is now ten o'clock. The choir will arrive for choir practice at three twenty, and evensong itself will be at four thirty."

"I see." Mr Gostelow made to leave. The stepladder was still propped against the chancel arch and, if someone should come into the church and interfere with it, he did not wish to be held responsible.

"One moment." The vicar gestured him to wait. "There is something else."

Mr Gostelow stared blankly at him and made no reply.

"It will probably not surprise you to know that one of the choirboys — Paul Mostyn — will not be attending today."

There was no response.

"Nor that there is a general feeling of sadness among members of the choir which I am sure you will respect."

"Will I?" The muscles in Mr Gostelow's jaw suddenly clenched. "Are you perhaps lecturing me, Mr Dalziel? Because, if you are, I think I should remind you that I have done nothing wrong. I behaved as any responsible, God-fearing man would have done, if he'd witnessed what I did."

"Really?" Mr Dalziel was by now less angry than upset. "And what exactly did you see?"

"You know very well," Mr Gostelow spat. "That Mostyn boy and the other one, Truett. Hanging around here when the others had left; holding hands when they thought no-one was looking. I watched them walking across the churchyard, and I saw them . . ." He paused as if unable to carry on. The muscles beneath one eye twitched convulsively. "I saw them — " He hissed the final word. "Kissing. Disgusting. An abomination. You know that as well as I do."

Mr Dalziel lowered his head. "I know," he said sadly, "that they were youngsters. What was required was calm and caring discussion."

"Calm and caring!" The church warden's tone was acid.

"Instead of which, you — *you*, Mr Gostelow, took it upon yourself, without consultation with anyone and with no regard for the boys' age and well-being, simply to confront both sets of parents and present them with a picture so distorted . . ."

"Distorted! I know what I saw and I did what was right. How dare you accuse me of distorting the facts!"

"Not the facts, Mr Gostelow. The interpretation of the facts. And it is not I who am accusing you."

For the first time Mr Gostelow's eyes betrayed a glimmer of uncertainty. "What do you mean?" he asked. "Who else . . . ?"

"I have been speaking with Mrs Mostyn, a lady not given to rash statements, and she is convinced you were in error. She tells me that her son is most persistent in his version of what occurred."

Any trace of doubt in Mr Gostelow rapidly vanished. "Of course," he snorted. "That's only to be expected."

Mr Dalziel dug his fingernails into the palm of his hand. "No," he said, more to himself than for the benefit of the unbending man in front of him. "No, Mr Gostelow, I shall not argue with you. But I *will* say this: I am deeply saddened that, after what has happened, you cannot find it in yourself to feel any pity or remorse."

"I did my duty as I saw it," Mr Gostelow said coldly. "It was not my fault that the boy lost his senses, and . . ." He stopped again.

"Yes?" Mr Dalziel said quietly. "And what?"

Mr Gostelow looked down on the vicar from his full height. When he spoke, every word was clear and hard-cut. "That the boy went and drowned himself," he said.

There was a long silence before the vicar spoke again. "There is no proof of that," he said. "It was a dark night; misty too. And the boy was confused. His parents are deeply shocked, with the inquest hanging over them as well."

"Yes," Mr Gostelow replied. "I am required to give evidence myself."

"The verdict, under the circumstances, will be one of

misadventure, I should think," the vicar said, choosing his words with great care.

"Possibly." The church warden turned to go. "Possibly, Vicar. But I would call it suicide myself."

The vicar ran his hand agitatedly through his meagre hair. He could hear the church warden stride back down the aisle, collect the ladder and haul it back to its rightful place. "Damn him," he thought. "Damn him and his unfeeling principles."

At two fifteen that afternoon, Mr Gostelow was in the kitchen of the church warden's cottage, arranging dirty saucepans in the sink. As he looked down the back garden, beyond the low hedge and into the field that rose slightly beyond, he was certain he could see a small, running creature bent low against the horizon. It dipped below the skyline then appeared further on, silhouetted against the pale clouds. Once more it disappeared and, this time, there was no further sign of it.

Odd. It had seemed the size of a small fox, but the movement was quite different. Sudden bursts of scurrying speed had been brought to a jerky halt as the creature seemed to find its bearings. Then it would scamper off along a new path. There were even times when it appeared to be moving only on its hind legs.

Mr Gostelow glanced at the kitchen clock: just over an hour before he was required back at the church. Time for a pot of tea and a chance to relax in front of the television. He placed the kettle on the hob and wandered through to the living room to make himself comfortable.

During the choir practice Mr Gostelow hovered on the

sidelines, making the necessary preparations for evensong: stacking hymn books and ensuring that there were enough hassocks for the congregation to kneel on. As he pottered back and forth, he debated telling the vicar about the damaged painting. He imagined Mr Dalziel's face on hearing that his precious masterpiece had been so irreparably damaged. "Such an unfortunate occurence," he could hear himself saying to the horrified vicar. "I thought I had better let you know as soon as possible." And he would keep a perfectly sincere face as he said it.

But any damage to the fabric of the building would bring the church warden himself into question. For if he was doing his job properly, supervising and locking up at the correct times, it should not have happened. There had, after all, been no signs of forced entry that he had seen. Better, under the circumstances, to wait, at least until the inquest business was over. When it had been established that he *had* simply been acting properly and responsibly; when the vicar was forced to eat humble pie, then he would tell him, and not before.

Thus, when Mr Dalziel arrived to conduct the service, only the briefest and most functional words passed between them. On such a cold winter's evening the choir almost outnumbered the congregation but the proceedings, if subdued, had at least been without incident. By six the church was locked, and Mr Gostelow began his homeward journey across the fields.

The sky was already night-black with no sign of a moon. Several times he had difficulty keeping his footing as he walked, and beneath his feet the earth felt like steel. He had no desire to slip and fall: it was quite possible that he would break a wrist or ribs. He slowed down and clung to the hedgerows. Some way off a creature called. It was a dismal cry, neither a screech nor a howl yet more unnerving than either. The sound soared towards him through the silent air. Stifling an involuntary shudder, he picked his way determinedly along the lines of frozen furrows.

It was with a feeling of relief that he reached the gate into his garden. He hurried down the path and let himself in through the back door.

The first thing he noticed was the foul smell: a stench of rotten, decayed food; sickly and pungent. There was nothing in the wastebin to produce such a smell. It was so strong he felt immediately nauseous. He must discover where it was coming from as quickly as possible. He pressed the light switch at his side.

Nothing happened.

As Mr Gostelow looked around the kitchen, he could see the shapes of familiar objects in the small blue glow of the pilot light on the stove. Feeling his way along the edge of the draining board he found the drawer containing useful odds and ends, and rummaged inside till he found the box of candles he knew was there. Taking one out, he manœuvred round the table to the cooker and placed the wick against the tiny flame. There was a slight delay, then a crackle as it caught light. Holding the candle in front of him he stepped into the hallway.

The dreadful smell was even more powerful than before. Impatiently he pushed open the living room door and pressed down the switch on the wall inside. Again there was nothing. The whole house must be blacked out. And that appalling smell. By now it reached into his throat and tore at his stomach. Where was it coming from?

He held the candle up, so that its light illuminated as much of the room as possible. The flame flickered and danced over the curtains, into corners and out again. He held it to the other side in order to see the wall directly opposite more clearly: the wall with the fireplace.

And then he saw it.

It squatted on the narrow mantelpiece watching him.

Its body had the colour and texture of stained leather and, with horrid fascination, Mr Gostelow watched the ribs rise and fall as it breathed, each gust of foetid air from its lungs like a choking wave in the confines of the small room. He saw the truncated arms and gnarled legs with their powerful talons; the face horned and beaked; and finally his eyes met those of the creature. They surveyed him unblinkingly.

Mr Gostelow gripped the candle tightly and froze. Something told him to make no sudden move; that he might yet be safe if only he could control himself. He moved slowly backwards fighting to keep command of his body, his breathing. Not for one fraction of time did he take his eyes off the creature, nor did its cold gaze ever leave his face.

At the moment he could feel the skirting board by the door with the back of his foot, he whirled abruptly and pushed through the doorway. There was a rush of air past his face. The candle wavered and as the flame steadied he gasped aloud. For there was the creature, crouched now on the staircase, halfway up, and peering at him through the rails of the banister.

Mr Gostelow let the candle drop. The demon's mouth opened, and from it issued forth poison and pestilence into his terrified face.

On the floor the candle spluttered and died.

"So you see, Mr Hopkins. We were not able to appoint anyone for a full six months: officially, he never left the post."

The two men stood outside the church in the warm sun of a May afternoon. Mr Dalziel was gazing across the fields towards the village. For a while the other man retained a diplomatic silence, but curiosity prevailed.

"You say this Mr Gostelow just left without telling anyone?"

The vicar continued to stare straight ahead but, Mr Hopkins noted, his eyes had focused on some nearer object. He appeared to be looking at a small headstone near the corner of the churchyard: a recent one to judge by the smooth, unweathered marble.

At last he blinked and said, "Yes. So it would seem. The Police discovered nothing of any use. Apparently, such cases of people going missing are by no means so uncommon as one would think. And, unless they decide to return, there is regrettably very little one can do. However — " He turned briskly and extended his hand. "The church cannot wait for ever on Mr Gostelow."

The two men shook hands and the vicar walked away down the path, leaving Mr Hopkins to assume his new duties. He entered the church and stood, savouring the atmosphere of this unusual building. Sunlight shafted in through the lancet windows, imbuing the stonework with its warmth.

Mr Hopkins looked up at the painting over the chancel arch. Somehow, on a day like this, it seemed aggressively out of place with its images of pain and torture and the little group of damned souls that cowered to one side. He examined them more closely. Whatever their sins, you couldn't help feeling a bit sorry for them.

One character in particular caught his eye: a tall, elderly figure at the back of the group, bent almost double with the weight of the triumphant demon astride his back. The head was twisted towards Mr Hopkins. It contained in its expression such a depth of anguish that he could not look at it for long.

He shook his head, dispelling this momentary feeling of depression, and strolled down the sunlit aisle towards the vestry.

Friends and Neighbours

I want to tell you about our next-door neighbours, and not just because they've been driving us crazy for the last ten years, although that'd be a good enough reason. It's just that something's happened and I've got to tell someone. My mate Pete knows about it, of course, but he's big and ugly so he doesn't really count.

Well, the woman who runs the looney-bin next door is called Mrs Mahoney. There used to be more inmates, but over the years they've sort of got whittled away. First to go was her husband, Ern. He was a big man with pipe wrenches for hands. Unfortunately, after a few pints in the Dog and Trumpet, he'd try to take people's heads off with them so he was put away. He comes out every now and then but he's soon back in. We reckon he prefers it in there: it's quieter for one thing.

Following in Dad's footsteps is something most fathers are dead chuffed about so, for all I know, Ern may be pleased with his kids. Brian's twenty and he's joined his dad in the nick; Steve's seventeen and in borstal; Colin's fourteen, and has just been taken into care for spray-painting half the town centre and decorating the Co-op's window display with a brick. And that leaves Mrs Mahoney and Clyde.

I call her Mrs Moany because whenever she's in our kitchen, begging for sugar or looking for gossip, that's all she seems to do:

"Do you know, I asked the milkman for three pints yesterday and when I opened the door there was only two. They says I said two but I never. Someone's been helping themselves, I says, and it might be the milkman or it might be them thieving brats from number twenty-two."

That's her usual sort of conversation; and notice it's always other people who do the nicking. I reckon she's got a faulty memory. The other thing you've probably guessed is that she's not very bright. If it starts raining when she's out shopping, she's the sort of person who'll put a bag on her head. Not a plastic bag, mind you, but a paper bag from Tesco's. So when she gets home she's got papier-mâché hair and blue stripes down her face.

Clyde's six, and he looks more like a human being than his brothers. That's the problem. I've told my mum she shouldn't be taken in by appearances but it's done no good. She thinks he's a little saint come to bless Mrs Moany in her old age after all the trouble she's had with her other kids. But I know different. After all, violence and vandalism runs in the blood, doesn't it? And you should see what he gets up to at home!

There's only a low hedge between our house and theirs, so it's dead easy to look over and into their kitchen. That's where most of the fun and games go on. Clyde's favourite trick is climbing on a stool, then up on to one of the kitchen units while his mum's upstairs. He'll wait there for ages by the door, quiet as death, then when his mum comes back in he'll clonk her on the head with whatever he's got in his hand. So far I've seen him use an egg whisk, a wooden spoon and even a frying pan (though he missed with that, thank God).

Now you may think, what's the problem? After all, we only hear the occasional yelp of pain through the wall and Clyde giggling. If that was true I'd sleep easy. But every Saturday Clyde comes on the wrong side of the wall — our side — while Mrs Moany goes to visit her old man, or one of the younger criminals.

Don't ask how it happened. Mum must have had a brainstorm when she offered to look after him. Correction: offered to let *me* look after him. That was four months ago and, for a long time after, I got these cold feelings down my spine every Friday night at the thought of another day with the Creature from the Black Lagoon. He only stays from ten in the morning till four o'clock, teatime, but he manages to pack a lot of unpleasantness into a short space so it seems longer. Let me give you some idea by telling you about the first time.

At five to ten there was a knock on the front door. When I opened it, there was Clyde on the doorstep, grinning. I went into the kitchen where Mum was getting the dinner ready.

"Guess what's arrived?" I said.

She glared at me, wiped her hands on a tea towel and swept me aside, saying, "Well, don't keep him waiting on the doorstep."

Only, by then, he was already halfway down the hallway.

"Oh. Hello, Clyde," Mum said.

"Hello, Mrs Parker," he smarmed, greasy as ever. He ignored me completely.

"I'm just getting dinner ready," Mum went on. "Andy will look after you." And she looked meaningfully at me.

That was how the nightmare began. During the rest of

the morning he played Tarzan, swinging from the curtains in my bedroom, and snapped the curtain rail; he found an old Action Man doll in my wardrobe and tried shoving it headfirst down the loo, and I didn't dare turn my back on him in case he nipped into Mum's room and pinched her jewellery.

Dinner was a gruesome affair, with Clyde doing his best to appear lovable. I only managed to control myself by imagining the things I'd like to do to him: crown him with the apple sauce bowl; tip gravy down the back of his trousers; stuff the roast potatoes up his nose. Afterwards, I had to help with the washing-up. It's a good job Mum never left me alone with him then. I'd got the newspaper headlines for the following day all worked out:

SIX-YEAR-OLD   MYSTERIOUSLY   DROWNS   IN
KITCHEN SINK

When all the crockery was back in the cupboards, Mum said, "Take Clyde into the living room. You can watch the television." I'll have to, I thought, otherwise he'll have it under his arm and out through the front door. As it happened, he was quite happy to sit there watching *World of Sport* — until I went upstairs to the loo.

You know those remote control things: the little box of buttons people use to change stations while they're doing their knitting? While I was out of the room, Clyde got his grubby paws on ours and decided it needed a workout. I came back to find the picture changing every couple of seconds like a speeded-up slide show. I just stood there, sort of mesmerised by the flashing pictures, then suddenly there was a crackle and a horse and jockey disappeared in a blinding flash.

I was still trying to see properly when Mum burst in. Clyde smiled and looked up at her. "Mrs Parker," he said. "I think there's something wrong with your telly."

She was a bit taken aback for a moment, then she stood him out in the hall while she had a go at me. "Wait till your dad comes home," she said. "He'll have a fit."

I'd already worked that out for myself, and I was all for packing my bags and leaving home there and then. Instead I had to suffer another couple of hours' torture with Clyde. By the time Mrs Moany picked him up at four, I was like a zombie. As for what happened when Dad came home, I don't want to talk about it: it's what you might call a painful memory.

Luckily, the television's rented. We had a man round from the Co-op on the Monday afternoon. When he fished out the circuit board at the back of the telly he seemed a bit surprised how much of it had melted, but he dropped another one in, downed a cup of tea and drove off. I was relieved, of course, but I'd still been put through the mincer for something I didn't do, and Clyde had wrecked my weekend.

That was the first time he paid us a visit. The Saturdays that followed were just as bad; I was steadily turning into a gibbering idiot. And I reckon the little white van would have come to collect me by now if I hadn't thought up my masterplan.

I figured the only way I'd ever have peace and regain my sanity was if he was carted off to join his brother, Colin, in care, but a six-year-old has to do something pretty drastic before that happens. Perhaps I could encourage him to set his house on fire. Knowing him, he'd jump at the chance. Trouble was, he'd probably burn ours down as well and then say that *I'd* done it. So that was no good. Anyway, I wouldn't really have played a dangerous trick like that, but just thinking about it made me feel a bit better.

Once I'd started thinking, though, I found I couldn't stop. My brain kept clicking round like a roulette wheel till, at last, the great idea dropped into place. Despite the fact that he was only six, Clyde was a little villain — there was no doubt about that — and he'd had plenty of chance to learn from his brothers, so he was good at it. You could bet he'd got a reputation among the boys at his school for thuggery and malice, and anyone who's proud of his reputation doesn't want to lose it. The one thing that would really take the wind out of his sails was if he suddenly found that his cronies didn't take him seriously any more, especially if they thought he was soft. And what do boys take the mickey out of each other about most? What do they reckon is soft? Girls, of course.

Now Pete Webb, who I told you about at the beginning, has a little sister called Mary. She's five and she's like Shirley Temple. She curtseys when she meets grown-ups for the first time and blows kisses through the front room window at the paperboy. Pete won't be seen dead with her because of the things his mates say. What's more, she and Clyde were at the same school. If his friends started to hear that Clyde went all gooey inside every time he saw Mary and love-hearts kept popping out of his eyes, they'd make his life a misery. Which was no more than he'd been doing to me. I might not get him out of my hair for good but at least I'd have the satisfaction of a bit of revenge.

How can you spread rumours quickly and make sure the right people find out? That had me flummoxed for a while. Then it came to me: Colin Moany's favourite toy — the spray-paint can. Only I wouldn't be wasting paint on things like MODS ARE COOL in four foot letters on the underpass. I'd choose my words, and where I put them, very carefully.

I got hold of the spray paint easy enough. The woman behind the counter gave me one of those We-know-what-you're-going-to-use-it-for looks as I handed over my money. Come to think of it, what else does anyone use it for? I just smiled charmingly and collected my change. Not that there was very much. I reckon vandals must be loaded: it's an expensive hobby. Once I'd smuggled it back into the house, all I had to do was wait.

That night, about eight o'clock, I told Mum I was just nipping round to Pete's and headed for Clyde's primary school instead. It's only a five minute walk so I was in no great hurry. I didn't want to look too suspicious. A good job too. I discovered something else that night: vandals are patient people. They have to be, if they don't want to be caught in the act.

When I walked past the first time, there was a kissing couple and they looked as though somebody'd welded them to the wall — and to each other for that matter. I waited round a corner twiddling my thumbs and counting the stars for ten minutes then, luckily, they decided to move. But slowly. It was another five minutes before they disappeared from view.

Hand on can, I popped my head round the corner, just in time to see a spaniel relieving itself up the brickwork.

Its owner was there too and gave me the same look as the woman in the shop. I decided to walk round the block.

When I got back the coast was clear. I didn't know for how long, though, so I had to work fast. Not too far up the wall, about where Clyde's head would have come, I wrote in big kiddy letters MARY 4 ME; then a bit further away CM 4 MW, and for good measure, at the end of the wall I put CLYDE L? They might only be primary school kids but they'd have to be as thick as an elephant's kneecap not to work that out. No-one had seen me, so I scarpered and waited to see what would happen.

It didn't take long. The following day I made sure I was home early, in time to see Clyde coming back from school. He looked like a different person. His grin had turned upside down, as if he'd just swallowed something very nasty and there was nowhere to spit it out. As he came through the front gate, he took a swipe at a rose bush with a twig he was carrying, but he'd sort of lost his energy and dropped the twig on the path.

I took a quick look through their kitchen window later and he wasn't even clouting his mum. Maybe I'd done her a favour as well. That night was the quietest we'd ever had. I chalked up a victory for psychology and went to bed happy.

Pete told me what had happened the following day. Mary had been full of it. Sure enough, everyone had seen the writing. His little gangster friends had decided he was an embarrassment and left him out of their games: kicking, thumping and betting behind the boiler room; and the girls had spent the whole day chasing him, hoping he'd join in their games, and trying to herd him towards Mary, who was loving every minute of it.

I was going to leave it at that. At least it had taught him some sort of lesson. He'd probably be back with his mates by the next week and it would all be forgotten, though for once he'd not had things all his own way. But one person wasn't satisfied yet: Mary. Clyde had managed to keep out of her way all week and her pride was hurt. She wanted to see him and find out what her shy admirer was like. Pete said she wouldn't stop talking about it. So, on balance, we decided he could suffer for a bit longer. We were going to arrange a meeting.

That Saturday, at nine o'clock, I asked Mum if I could go round to Pete's.

"You know Clyde's coming," she said.

"Yes," I replied. "Maybe I could take him too."

"Maybe," she said, eyeing me suspiciously. "How do I know the two of you won't bully him?"

"Because Mary'll be there too, and if we did she'd tell you."

Mum laughed. "You're probably right there. OK, but not for too long."

So far, so good. I didn't think it would take very long.

When Clyde arrived I turned him straight round, dragged him up the path and out of the gate.

"What are you doing?" he yelled, scuffing his heels on the pavement.

"We're going to see a friend of mine, but don't worry — there'll be someone for you to talk to as well."

"Who? What's his name?"

"Wait till we get there," I said, "and you can ask for yourself."

Pete's mum was out shopping, and he had everything ready as planned. Once in the house, we steered Clyde into the living room where Mary was waiting with her rosy cheeks and ringlets. Then Pete and I nipped out smartish and held the door handle, in case he tried doing a bunk.

"Oi," cried a muffled voice from inside. Then he tried the door. "Let me out. That girl's in here."

"She only wants to say hello," I shouted back. "Just be nice to her for five minutes."

"Get stuffed!"

I was just trying to work out a suitable reply when there was suddenly a hefty smack at the bottom of the door. "Let me out," he yelled, "or I'll kick the door in!"

I believed him.

Pete groaned. "Oh no. My mum'll kill me."

I believed that as well. Mrs Webb was built like a bison. It was best not to get her angry. So we let go of the handle, waited till Clyde opened the door, then pounced on him and sat him down on the sofa. With me holding one arm and Pete the other, he wasn't going very far. Mind you, we had to sit at an odd angle, to keep out of range of his feet which he was thrashing around like club hammers.

All this time Mary sat in a corner, looking a bit paler than usual. "You're horrid," she announced suddenly. She could've meant me and Pete, I suppose, but she was staring straight at Clyde.

Clyde grinned unpleasantly. To him that was a compliment. Then he blew a long and revolting raspberry. Clearly, this wasn't going to be the beginning of a beautiful friendship. All we were doing was helping him back into his gangster role; and Mary wasn't going to play Bonnie. I might as well take the little monster home.

Just then Mary stood up. She walked over to the sofa,

staying just far enough away to avoid the hammers, then she lifted back her right arm so fast I hardly saw it happening. Next second she'd landed Clyde a slap on the cheek you could've heard at Land's End. Her face had got its colour back now all right. She hissed at him, "Don't do that!" Then she clouted him again, just as hard on the same cheek. As his head bounced back towards her, she stared him in the eye and said, ever so quietly, "And I'll tell you what you can do. You can piss off!" Then she ran out of the room and up the stairs.

If someone had taken a picture of us sitting there, you'd have thought we were window dummies. I couldn't move for shock and Pete had his mouth open so far you could see all his fillings. We'd both let go of Clyde, so he could've done anything — torn the place apart if he'd wanted to. Instead he just sat there. I think he was more confused than anything.

And suddenly he began to cry. That's what surprised me most of all. I mean, you don't expect an evil monstrosity to do something like that. I almost felt sorry for him. But, even while the tears were bubbling down his face, I knew what I had to do. I could stop him making my life a misery once and for all, even if I did feel a bit of a rat for doing it.

"Clyde," I said.

He was blowing his nose on his sleeve now. He didn't seem in a hurry to answer.

"Clyde, if you don't sort yourself out, all your mates are going to find out what just happened."

That's what I was going to say, but somehow I felt such a bully all of a sudden that I couldn't bring myself to. He was lost in his own little world and probably wouldn't have heard me anyway.

"Come on, Clyde," I said. "Let's go home."

As we left I turned to Paul. "I never knew your sister had a forearm smash like that."

"Neither did I. Nor the language to go with it."

"I guess you've got to be a bit careful with women."

"Yeah." He smiled. "Look after Clyde there. Even Big Daddy would've been out for the count after that."

We walked home in silence.

The rest of that day Clyde sat in front of the telly and hardly moved. Mum tried to find out what happened, but I wasn't ready to tell her and Clyde wasn't saying anything.

After he'd gone home I tried to explain, but it wasn't easy. For one thing, I'd no intention of admitting I was a first-degree vandal. We expected Mrs Moany to turn nasty, but all that happened was that Clyde started trekking off with her on Saturdays. She still came round to borrow things but not so often, and she left sooner than she used to.

Then last week we heard they were moving. To start with I thought it was my fault, not that I'd have minded too much. But then we found out she'd been on the council housing exchange list for years. Seems she wanted to move to London for family reasons. I suppose she thought sooner or later they'd all be in prison there so she'd better get as near as possible. Now we've got some new people moving in.

As for Clyde, I couldn't honestly say I'm sorry to see the back of him, but I have been thinking about him a bit. It can't be a cosy life having a dad who's in the nick, three crazy brothers and a dopey mum. It'd be a bit surprising if he was an angel, wouldn't it? I mean, he's had the odds against him from the start.

Talking of odds, I've got a bet on with Pete about our new neighbours. I saw them looking round the other day and they've got a daughter, about my age as it happens. She's got blonde hair and tight jeans, and the bet is: who goes out with her first? It's like taking candy from a baby really — what with me having natural charm and good looks, and Pete being big and ugly. Trouble is, he thinks he's not.

I'm looking forward to playing some new Tarzan games up in the bedroom! I wonder if her name's Jane.

The Keeper of the Key

At nearly seven o'clock in the evening, the empty school seemed twice its normal size. It also doubled any noise: footstep; breathing; heartbeat. The figure in jeans and trainers waited in the darkened room, counting the seconds. Silently, the room waited too. During the day it hummed quietly but now everything was switched off.

Then the overhead lights flickered quickly before beaming full upon the twenty computers and the figure with the crowbar.

With the door firmly closed, there was little chance of being heard. But the dustcovers could stay on too: they'd help deaden the sound. The crowbar came up, almost level with the lights. The hand holding it hovered in mid-air. Suddenly the room seemed full of hooded heads, silent in mechanical prayer.

Blinking away this image, the tensed figure concentrated, eyes closed, drew in a deep breath and unlocked the frozen bar into a descending arc. It ploughed downwards, cracking the plastic skull beneath, shattering the glass and burying itself in delicate brain circuits. Magnified by the hollow room, the sound that emanated from the savaged machine was appalling.

Its attacker moved to the next one. The first had been the most difficult; the rest would be progressively easier.

Ten minutes later the room was again silent.

Monday

The kitchen was still in darkness when Mrs Charters came downstairs at six. She peered through the slats of the Venetian blind. Outside a thin, grey dawn was filtering from the horizon into the black sky above. Neither winter nor spring: she hated this time of year.

It was not until she had put the kettle on the stove and lit the first cigarette of the morning that she remembered the calendar needed to be changed. She crossed to the strip of wall by the door, where it hung, and tore off February's picture of an Airedale Terrier along its serrated edge. March sported a poodle

Mrs Charters threw the Airedale into the pedal bin by the sink, flicked cigarette ash on top of it and clacked the lid back down.

The living room was darker still. Thick curtains wiped out the dawn light. When Mrs Charters opened the door and stepped in, it reminded her of the cinema: secluded darkness, the tang of stale cigarette smoke on the air. For a moment she left the light off. Once upon a time, too long ago to be part of this life, they had gone out to the cinema often.

She clicked the switch, squinting as the triple light in the centre of the ceiling burst white. She picked up the full ashtray from next to the armchair facing the television. Everything, sooner or later, burned down to ash.

The tiny red light at the bottom of the television was still glowing. How had she not seen it when she opened the door? The armchair must have been blocking her view. George must have forgotten to switch it off properly; just pressed the remote control button on the handset and watched the picture fragment before coming up to bed. She'd been asleep of course. Not that it would have made much difference one way or the other.

She stared at the pinpoint of red. No sense in putting it off now. Sooner or later he'd be down to watch breakfast TV. More TV than breakfast. He'd take a cup of coffee through from the kitchen, light a cigarette and click — the day would begin.

Mrs Charters pulled back the curtains a short way. A pillar of pale sky rose between the dark folds. She crossed the room, switched off the lights and went back to the kitchen. Zoe was standing by the sink.

"Hello, love. Didn't expect you down yet." Mrs Charters stopped just inside the doorway. "How long have you been up? I didn't hear you."

Zoe yawned. "I just woke up early, that's all. Before the alarm went off. No point in trying to get back to sleep. Anyhow, I hate the noise that thing makes. I'd rather be awake before it starts ringing."

Her mother half smiled. "Wait till you get to my age. I seem to wake up earlier each day. And at the weekend. Can't even enjoy a good lie-in these days."

Zoe switched off the gas. "Cup of tea, Mum?"

"Yeah. Make a pot, love. Be just you and me, mind."

"Dad not awake yet?"

Mrs Charters busied herself with the cups and saucers. For another two minutes neither of them spoke. They did not feel uncomfortable. Silence was the natural order of things.

" 'Ere, Gaz. Look who's on gate duty today."

"Prat!" Gary Deakin spat on the pavement. He was a tall, athletic boy with a permanently aggressive jaw that softened only when he was a long way from school.

Standing by the driveway, just the other side of the metal gates at the school entrance, stood Mr Jeal, the Senior Master and overseer of boys' discipline, a role he liked to exercise with an iron hand. He was widely hated and despised; sometimes feared. Any pupils who respected him did so in the same way that they would respect a scorpion. And, in the same way, they stayed well out of striking range.

The small group of fifth year boys slowed down. "No chance of an extra fag now," one of them complained.

" 'Ere, Andy," another one said, loud enough for Mr Jeal to hear. "Where's the ciggies? Go on, bung 'em over."

Mr Jeal's mouth tightened and he stared blankly in the other direction. Gary thumped the boy who'd spoken. "Watch it, Phil," he grunted. "All we need is for him to start poking around in the bags, you stupid sod."

A few moments later and the little group was strolling nonchalantly into school. Mr Jeal waited until the boys drew level.

"Gary, wait a minute."

The group carried on walking.

"Gary!"

Let him raise his voice. Push his blood pressure up a bit. Early morning aggravation was always the most effective. Slowly Gary and his friends stopped, but none of them turned to look at Mr Jeal.

"The rest of you can go," he said testily. "Gary's the only one I asked to see. Hard of hearing this morning, eh Gary?"

Gary said nothing. The other boys stayed where they were.

"I said off you go!" The voice was raised again. The little muscles at the corner of Mr Jeal's eyes twitched, pulling the yellow-grey bags beneath into new creases. The other boys traipsed slowly down the path towards the school buildings. Senior Master and pupil faced each other.

"Well, Gary," Mr Jeal continued, more comfortable now the others had moved beyond earshot. "So you like a cigarette in the morning, do you?"

Gary shook his head and frowned, convincingly puzzled. "No, sir."

"So I'm hearing things, am I?"

"Pardon, sir?"

"The conversation. About cigarettes."

Gary shook his head noncommittally. "I don't think anyone mentioned my name."

"So you don't?"

"What?"

"Smoke."

The twitching was there again, however much he tried to pretend calm. Gary fixed his gaze on a point somewhere between Mr Jeal's right eye and ear, and said nothing.

"All right. Open your bag."

Gary sighed, unzipped the blue sports bag at his feet and carefully removed every item, laying it out on the ground at the Senior Master's feet. No cigarettes. He straightened up and grinned. "Disgusting habit: smoking."

Mr Jeal silently motioned him to put the things away again, and hurriedly left to confront a small boy riding his bike through the gateway. "Walk!" he boomed. "Get off and push it. You know the rules."

Gary picked up the bag and walked away. Good job the old fool only had it in for him. The other bags would have proved a much more profitable source of investigation. He glanced down at the lettering on the bag swinging at his side. *Chelsea* it said. As if he'd support a crummy team like that. Still, if Jeal would insist on looking in the opposite direction as they came into school, what did he expect? Phil could have his bag back during registration.

Sometimes it was all too easy.

"I can't do this sodding computer program."

The complaint sliced through the antiseptic calm of the computer room. It came from a girl in the corner. She was staring sullenly at the screen in front of her. For a moment heads turned, then most of the class resumed tackling their own problems; all except one boy two seats away. "Shouldn't be in this group then, should you, Linda?" he said.

Linda glared round the shoulder of the girl next to her. "Thank you, Brian," she grated through clenched teeth. "We all knew you were a boff, but I didn't realise you were a bitch as well!"

Brian made a miaowing noise and carried on with his work.

Linda stood up, quietly determined, and moved menacingly towards him. Enough was enough. "Try taking your bifocals off, Einstein, and say that again."

At that moment Mr Carr chose to look up from his desk.

"Linda," he warned. "Sit down, please."

"Christ," she muttered under her breath. "Don't tell me he's alive." The girl next to her laughed.

Mr Carr was stung into action. He was a comparatively young man, about thirty-five, but already he gave the impression of impending middle-age. It was a mystery to most pupils how anyone with more hair on his chin than the top of his head could take himself so seriously, let alone expect others to. But he was a proud man and laughter wounded him easily.

"What do you think you're laughing at, Beverley?" he demanded, striding towards the scene of the trouble.

"Typical," Linda whispered. "He'll come over here to tell you off, but try and get him to help you with your work . . ."

"Well, Beverley?" he asked again. He was standing between the two girls.

Beverley shrugged her shoulders. "Dunno, sir."

"What do you mean — 'Don't know'? You must have a reason for laughing."

She contemplated telling him it was his flared trousers or the enormous lapels on his grubby jacket. Instead she looked as blankly innocent as possible and said nothing.

"It was my fault, sir," Linda interrupted. "I was trying to get your attention but you didn't seem to hear me."

Beverley swung back round on her swivel chair and began to attack her keyboard with renewed vigour. Mr Carr was compelled to talk to Linda.

"Well?" he said. "What's the problem?"

"It's this program, sir. I can't make it work."

"Well, the computer can't think for itself; it's not intelligent. That's where you come in. You've clearly made an error in the program itself."

Linda shot him a despairing glance. "I know. That's

what I'm trying to tell you. I can't work out how to do this bit of the program."

"They say," Brian announced from two seats away, "that the Fifth Generation computers will be able to — think for themselves that is. What's your opinion, sir? Do you reckon artificial intelligence is only a short step away?"

"Well, Brian, that's an interesting hypothesis. It all depends what you actually mean by intelligence."

He moved along the table and began an earnest conversation with his star pupil. Linda knifed him in the back with her eyes.

"See what I mean?"

Beverley smiled sympathetically.

On the far side of the room Zoe had been busy with something else: her bag. To begin with the search had been quite routine, a casual check. But for the last two minutes she had been foraging frantically inside the pockets of the bag. Finally she re-zipped it and sat quietly, her hands on her lap.

"What's up?" the boy next to her asked.

She brushed the question quickly aside. "Nothing. It's all right thanks."

She scrutinised the other pupils in the room. Most of them were in the fifth year. She and a boy named Laurence, a tall, gangly individual with acne, were the only sixth formers present. It was their free period of the day. Both were in the 'A' level Computer Studies' group, and needed to put in as much time as possible on programming. This was particularly true for Zoe: unlike the others in her group she had no facilities at home. That was the main reason Mr Carr had let her have a key to the room as well.

"I shouldn't really," he'd said. "Security risk and all that, but if you really want to put in some time after school . . ."

"It would help. I find it difficult keeping up with the others."

"And there's no chance of you getting one of your own?"

She tried hard to bite back her pride. "Things are a bit difficult at the moment. What with my dad being out of work and that. It would have been easier if I hadn't stayed on, of course."

"No, no" Mr Carr had said hurriedly — embarrassed. "I quite understand. Well, we don't need to tell anyone. As it happens I do have a spare key. So long as you let me have it back during school holidays . . ."

"Thank you. I'll be very careful with it."

And now she would have to tell him it had gone.

The computer conference at the other side of the room had come to an end. Mr Carr was walking back to his desk. Should she catch his eye now? Explain quietly under cover of asking a question about her work? No. Not with the others in the room. Wait. Be patient. There were only ten minutes left till Breaktime.

For the remainder of the lesson the only noise was the clatter of fingers on keyboards; quiet electronic conversation within the computers; then the shuffling of feet and bags on the anti-static carpet as the group prepared to leave. All except Brian. He was still engrossed in his work. Zoe frowned. She didn't want him around to complicate matters. Fortunately Mr Carr himself came to the rescue.

"Any of you wanting to carry on during Break, I'm

afraid I'm going to have to disappoint you," he announced. "I have to lock up while I attend a short meeting in the staffroom."

"Oh dear," Beverley said. "What a shame." She turned to Brian, who had begun to tut complainingly. "Never mind, dear. You'll have to make do with conversation for twenty minutes. *You* know? How people communicate with each other when they haven't got their heads buried in microchips."

"Huh!" Brian sneered.

"Not bad," Beverley said. "For a first attempt. Hey, Linda, did you hear that? Now I know how a mother feels when her baby says its first word. Not Mama or Dada — just Huh! We'll see if we can get him on to proper words next week."

"You cow!" Brian spat at her. He was getting flustered now.

"Quick developer," Beverley confided once again to Linda. "See, he's on to words of one syllable already."

Linda, for her part, stopped laughing long enough to ask, "Do you think he might even be intelligent, then?"

Beverley adopted her thoughtful expression. "Hm. Too early to tell really. But they do say that the Fifth Generation Boffin will be able to think for himself. What do you reckon, Linda?"

"Damn you!" Brian stood up and grabbed Beverley's shoulder.

From the safety of his desk, Mr Carr called "What's going on?"

Very quietly Beverley hissed, "Get your hand off my shoulder, little boy." He did. She turned round on her chair, smiling broadly for Mr Carr's benefit. "Nothing serious, sir. Just mucking around. Once more, though," she said gently to Brian, "and I'll be in to see Mrs Mallory before you can say 'sexual harassment'. And I've got a witness."

"That's right," Linda said.

He looked as if he might cry, but at that moment the bell rang for the end of the lesson. For once Brian was first out of the room. The others bustled after him, and within a minute the room was empty except for Mr Carr and Zoe.

"Come along," he chided her. "I don't want to be late."

"Er, Mr Carr?"

"What's the matter?"

"Would you mind closing the door for a minute?"

"Pardon?"

"There's something I want to tell you."

He closed the door and waited. "What about?" His expression was one of surprise and annoyance combined.

"I've lost my purse."

If anything, he appeared relieved. "Oh," he said smiling. "Well, I'm sorry but lost property isn't really my affair. Was there much in it?"

"About three pounds . . . and the key."

She watched his face change. "What?" he said quietly. "You mean . . ."

"Yes, sir. The key to the computer room."

"You're sure?" he demanded.

"I checked and double-checked. The purse was in my bag when I came to school this morning; I'm sure it was. But it's not there now." She dutifully emptied the contents on his desk to make the point.

"So are you saying it's been stolen?"

"I don't know, sir."

"Well, you've only had the one lesson today. It could have been someone in the group. Why didn't you tell me before they left? We could have searched everyone."

Zoe looked despondent. "I'm sorry, sir. I didn't want to tell you in front of everyone else. I mean, no-one else knows I had a key, do they?"

Mr Carr began to twist strands of his beard between thumb and forefinger. He sighed. "Yes that's true. Well, is there any other way it could have gone missing?"

"I've been thinking about that. Yes, there is. I left my bag in the cloakroom for ten minutes during registration. I didn't think — for ten minutes — it ought to have been OK."

Mr Carr didn't have to speak. His face said exactly what he thought of her. As he contemplated what to do he drummed his fingers on the desk. "Right," he said at last. "First you go and see Mr Jeal. He's the man in charge of lost property. It *may* be that the purse has been found. At any rate, he has to be told it's missing. And let's hope whoever took it was only interested in the money."

The thought cheered him a little. "Yes. That's probably it. We'll just have to hope that the purse and the other items in it turn up soon. I'd better have a word with Mr Jeal as well, to explain why you had a key in the first place." He sighed again deeply.

Zoe scooped her belongings back into her bag. "I'll go and see him now then, shall I?"

Mr Carr crossed to the door, opened it and ushered her into the corridor before locking it again. "Yes. And keep your fingers crossed while you're at it."

Zoe walked down the corridor slowly, planning exactly

what to say. Mr Jeal was totally unpredictable. He might seethe and storm, or he might equally well say, 'Never mind, dear. Tell me all about it.' It depended on his mood and how much you were prepared to roll your eyes at him. On balance, Zoe decided not to degrade herself. She would let him have the facts and he could like it or lump it.

There was a sudden loud whistle from behind, followed rapidly by noises of throaty lust. She looked dismissively over her shoulder. Gary Deakin and friends had appeared out of nowhere and were lounging against the wall. Under her wilting glance the noise stopped; but as soon as her back was turned, there they were, at it again.

"Cor, she's a bit of all right, i'nt she?"

"D'you reckon she would, eh?"

"Go on, ask 'er, Andy."

" 'Ere, gorgeous, what you doin' tonight?"

Hadn't she got enough problems without this drooling bunch of adolescents making an exhibition of themselves? She braced herself to stop and say something. Then another voice in the group spoke. "Lay off," it said. "You don't have to be a yob all the time, for Christ's sake."

Zoe smiled. A human being! Things were looking up. She turned the corner to wait outside Mr Jeal's office.

"What's got into you today?" Andy complained.

"Not a lot," Gary said. "I just reckon you should take a few lessons in subtlety, that's all."

"She's not a bad bit of stuff though, is she?" Phil put in.

"Not a bad bit of stuff?" Gary echoed incredulously. "Good God, you're as bad as him." He poked Andy in the chest to make his point more forcibly. "You don't even bother to look above the waist, do you?"

He pictured the girl's walk: legs, hips. Of course she was attractive. But they weren't the only reasons. She had a way of looking at people that he'd noticed before, relaxed and in control. He admired that.

"Come on," Phil said. "Let's get outside. My lungs are suffering from nicotine withdrawal. You comin', Romeo?" He grinned broadly at Gary.

Gary regarded him quizzically. "You never told me you were fond of hospital food, Phil." His voice was dangerously quiet.

Together they strolled off. Gary was at the front.

"Well, young lady. What can I do for you?"

Mr Jeal was a plump, unpleasant man. His skin gleamed, permanently moist, and thin whisps of ginger hair clung damply to his otherwise bald scalp. Shirts which fitted his neck and shoulders bulged at the middle, making little windows between the tightly-stretched buttons, through which peeped his pallid stomach.

At the moment he was closing his appointments diary and looking up at her with what might also have passed for a friendly smile. Zoe launched into her speech.

"I've lost my purse, and Mr Carr said I should tell you. I think it was taken from my bag during registration. I left it in the cloakroom."

"I see. Is your name in the purse?"

Here we go, she thought. All the routine nonsense questions. Every single thing you brought to school was supposed to be labelled: socks, shoes, purse, knickers! Had Mr Jeal ever tried writing in a purse she wondered. Maybe he had, come to think of it. She could imagine him as a schoolboy, inscribing all his belongings: Maurice

Jeal, The Hawthorns, Hollyberry Lane, Anytown, England, The World, The Universe. That sort of person never grew up, especially if he worked in a school.

"No, there were a few odds and ends in it. Something might have had my name on it but I don't think so." What about the key? Should she mention that? Mr Carr had already volunteered to explain. There was no need to put her head on the block as well.

"There was about three pounds in it," she added quickly, and hoped he'd enquire no further.

He shrugged his shoulders. "Well, it may turn up: the purse that is. I should think you've seen the last of the money. Check at home to make sure you didn't leave it there by mistake. It's easily done. If you don't have any luck, see me again tomorrow and I'll put it in the morning announcements. OK?"

"Thank you," Zoe said quietly. She backed deferentially out of the office. The encounter had been brief and relatively painless. Only one thing troubled her: would Mr Carr do as he had said? Well. There was no point in worrying about that now.

Every room in the Deakins' house belonged in an illustrated catalogue. The kitchen gleamed new, though it was two years since Gary's father had redesigned and rebuilt it. The living room was lit by subtly placed spotlights, and velvet cushions lay scattered, not at random but in the right places, to create the impression of careless luxury. The house itself was a semi-detached on a small, private estate, but extensions here, a new porch there, and the finishing touches of Mrs Deakin's interior design singled it out as a house of quality.

Gary hated it.

He took every opportunity to sabotage its inhuman tidiness. That was why he now dug his trainers into the material of the settee as he sprawled across it, watching the television. He leaned forward slightly to catch the words: the sound was turned down low.

When the phone rang, he was in the hall before his mother could appear at the kitchen door. "I'll get it," he shouted. He stopped and made himself count two more rings before picking up the receiver. It might not, after all, be for him.

"Hello?" he said hoarsely. "72941 . . . Yeah, just watching telly . . . No, nothing special. Had a bit of a run-in with old Jeal this morning by the gate. He's definitely got it in for me. So, what's new at your end? . . . Yeah? So far so good then, eh?"

He leaned against the wall, glancing occasionally towards the kitchen door as he concentrated on the voice at the other end. For a further two minutes he made no interruption until — "Yeah, sure. You make it sound like a doddle." He laughed; abruptly stopped; listened again. "Yeah. Same here. When will I . . . ? No, all right . . . Oh, I'll think of something — tell her it was a wrong number that wouldn't take no for an answer. Right. Bye then."

He replaced the receiver and was halfway across the hall when his mother's voice called from the kitchen, "Who was it?"

He smiled at the predictability of her response. Foolish even to imagine he could reach the relative safety of the living room before she asked. "Oh, just Phil," he called back. "Wants to know if I fancied a game of squash down the Leisure Centre. He's got a court booked."

"Are you going?"

"No. I'm busy enjoying this film. He'll have to find someone else for tonight."

The silence on the other side of the door signalled an end to the conversation. He went back to the settee and turned up the volume on the television.

Gary, he thought: you're a born liar. Thank God!

Tuesday

Zoe checked her watch against the clock in the front room before leaving the house. It was, unfortunately, the most reliable timepiece they had, otherwise she would not have gone near it. It made her remember things she did not want to remember.

"It's an insult," he'd shouted. "A bloody insult. What did they think they were bloody playing at?"

"They couldn't have known. I'm sure they wouldn't do it on purpose." Mrs Charters tried to calm her husband. He was standing in the centre of the room, a cardboard box and chunks of polystyrene packing strewn on the sofa; in his hand the carriage clock.

Zoe was on the floor where she'd been lying reading a comic. She watched his hands, fascinated. It seemed to her that they wanted to crush the clock, the fingers were closed so tightly round the polished case.

"Plastic and batteries. Brushed aluminium and a bit of cheap brass. When my dad finished work, they gave him a beautiful gold watch. I've got it upstairs in the drawer." Was he talking to himself, or maybe to the hated clock in his hand? His voice was choked and strange.

"Now then, George," Mrs Charters said gently.

His eyes flamed with anger. "At least it wasn't put together on a bloody conveyor belt," he shouted.

Zoe was frightened. Sometimes, when he was like this, things happened. It was not simply that he lost control; his temper became a violent creature suddenly uncaged. It had a mind of its own. She waited for him to hurl the clock across the room or dash it to bits against the mantelpiece. Instead he gasped as if some unseen fist had punched all the breath out of him.

Then he cried. Slow tears had crawled down his face as he stood, motionless, in the middle of the floor. And Mrs Charters had taken the clock from his loosened fingers and placed it carefully on the mantelpiece. There it had stayed ever since.

Zoe had been twelve, but she could still not look at the clock without remembering. And usually, unless she tried very hard to think quickly of something else, another incident elbowed its way forward from the back of her memory; a conversation this time.

"It didn't have a face, you see."

"What? A clock with no face?"

"That's right."

"So where were its hands?"

"No face and no hands either."

"Are you telling the truth?"

For, as a little girl, she had never been quite sure. He told her whopping, straight-faced lies, then chortled with laughter when she believed him. She'd learnt to tell when he was doing that, because her mother would always make a little tutting noise with her mouth and look away. Only this time her mother wasn't there; just the two of them in the living room before she went up to bed.

"So how did people see the time?"

"With their ears."

"Silly!" she giggled.

"You don't believe me, do you?"

"No."

"It's true. They didn't have watches in those days, so when they went on a long journey they carried a small clock with them. And what do you think they were riding in at the time?"

He made a clip-clop noise.

"Horses?"

"I said *in*, not *on*." He tickled her for getting it wrong. "Carriages, that's what. And because they travelled all through the night the carriages were very dark. So it was no good having a clock with a face and hands when you couldn't even see your own hand in front of your face. You had a small clock in a case and, when you wanted to know the time, you pulled a string at the side. That rang the bell, and the number of times the little bell rang told you which quarter of an hour you were nearest to. That was all they wanted to know in those days. They weren't in a hurry. People didn't bother much about minutes and seconds — before the world speeded up."

And the story, which had been a silly story, a happy story, had felt suddenly sad to Zoe. Often, after that, she would lie in bed and imagine herself in a darkened carriage with the night for company and the sound of small bells to ring her to sleep.

Mr Jeal prided himself on his punctuality. Every morning, before eight o'clock, he arrived at his parking spot near the main entrance and, as school didn't officially begin till a quarter to nine, that usually made him the first on the premises. It was a good feeling. For a while, at least, it was *his* school.

This was a view not shared by Mr Duke, the caretaker, whose squat bungalow sat just inside the school grounds. He was the one who got up at six in the morning; he was the one who had to deal with blocked drains, tennis balls lobbed on to the roof and general rudeness from the little criminals who propped themselves against his garden fence every day. Teachers! Most of them didn't know they were born, rabbitting on inside their cosy classrooms. When all eight hundred children exploded out of the building at the end of the day, where were the teachers then, he wanted to know: in the staffroom huddled round the electric kettle, or leaping into their cars with the speed of escaping bank robbers.

He stopped setting out bollards round a recently arrived rubbish skip and watched the Senior Master clamber out of his car, briefcase in hand. Mr Jeal noticed him and flashed an immediate chummy smile.

"Morning, Jack," he called over.

Mr Duke did not reply. Only his friends called him Jack. When people in charge tried calling you by your christian name, it meant one thing and one thing only: they were trying to con you. Pretend everyone was equal — all part of a team, and let's be buddy-buddy. Mr Duke had no intention of being any member of staff's buddy, least of all Mr Jeal's.

He dropped another plastic cone to the ground with a thump.

Mr Jeal was not in the least put out by the caretaker's offhand manner. He simply ignored it. "Bit nippy this morning, Jack," he said and carried on walking.

"Just a minute, Mr Jeal."

"Yes?"

"Got something here I thought you should take a look at." He fished inside the pocket of his baggy grey overall and pulled out a large purse. "Diane, the girl who cleans the science block, gave it me last night before she left. Says she found it in one of the bins. Biology lab, I think it was. Anyway, it was stuffed right at the bottom of the bin. We reckoned it had probably been nicked."

He pushed it at Mr Jeal's spare hand. Mr Jeal took it and looked it over, put down his briefcase, opened the purse and frowned. "Nothing in it?" he asked.

Mr Duke snorted. "You must be bloody joking. Get rid of the evidence, that's what they do isn't it? They get enough practice in this place!"

Mr Jeal seemed about to argue, but changed his mind. "I don't think so," he said curtly.

"Oh, come off it." Mr Duke was not going to let him off the hook so readily. "Coats go missing; money vanishes. You should know: lost property and all that. Purloined property more like." He chuckled at his own joke and the annoyance he knew it would cause Mr Jeal.

"If that's all — ?" Mr Jeal picked up his briefcase and headed for his room.

"For now," Mr Duke called cheerfully after him. "Till

the next time." And he began to whistle as he plonked down another bollard.

Mr Hamilton taught English, but not very well. It wasn't that he didn't try; in fact, he was most conscientious about preparing his lessons and marking work. Unfortunately, older pupils had a way of getting under his skin, so that what began as a discussion of *Day of the Triffids* ended as a stand-up argument.

His fifth year group was only too aware of this weakness and, as they had been with him now for four terms, had turned winding him up into a fine art. Occasionally they would time the process to remind themselves how fast it could be done. The record was six minutes and today it looked like being broken. Barely three minutes into the lesson, Mr Hamilton was already in danger of bursting a blood vessel.

"You what!" he bellowed.

"I didn't do it. We went out last night, see."

The sustained volume of Mr Hamilton's voice warned of imminent volcanic eruption. "What you did last night has nothing to do with it. You've had two weeks to complete this project — two weeks!"

Gary Deakin grinned over the desk at one of the girls in the group. Mr Hamilton's dignity was in danger of collapsing like a punctured airbed.

"Look at me when I'm talking to you," he screeched.

Gary looked at him.

"I want a proper explanation."

"I just told you," Gary replied casually, and leaned back to balance on the two back legs of his chair. Mr Hamilton heard noises of unrest behind him and began to panic. He could not afford a confrontation that he might lose.

"I'll give you one more chance."

"Don't bother," Gary retorted. "I'm not going to do it anyway."

Mr Hamilton rocked on his heels. It was a sign the class knew well. Not much longer now. The next phase was the deadly quiet threat.

"Gary." There was menace in his whisper. "You have just made a big mistake."

"I know. I came to your lesson. They're always boring as hell. That's why I didn't do your homework, if you really want to know."

"How dare you!" Mr Hamilton yelled. "Get out. Go on! Go and see Mr Jeal. I've had enough of your insolence . . ." He ground to a momentary halt.

"OK," Gary agreed, stood up, swung his bag over his shoulder and quietly left.

"Four minutes twenty seconds," he heard someone say admiringly.

A promising start to the day.

Mr Jeal had been about to deal with the purse and its vanished contents when Gary Deakin turned up outside his room. Half an hour later, after a heated conference with Mr Hamilton and an equally heated exchange with Gary himself on the subject of a week's detentions, he was back in his office. One day he'd get that boy, not for some triviality like rudeness to a teacher, but for something big: something he could really nail him on. When he wanted, Mr Jeal could be a patient man.

Spread on the desk in front of him was a copy of the

sixth form timetable; according to that, Zoe Charters was nearing the end of a Chemistry lesson. He buzzed the office and asked the secretary to go and fetch her. Five minutes later she arrived.

"Is it about my purse?" she asked him.

"Yes. We've found it."

"Really?"

"But I was right about the contents: they've gone."

Her face fell. "What? Everything?"

"Yes. It would have been a little unrealistic to expect the money to be there still."

"Well — " She stopped, uncertain.

He was in like a whippet. "Was there something else then?"

"I thought — didn't Mr Carr come to see you yesterday? He said he was going to."

"No. What should he come to see me for?"

"About the key — to the computer room."

The beginnings of several expressions half-formed on Mr Jeal's face in rapid succession. Eventually he settled for one of subdued shock.

"Are you saying there was such a key in your purse?"

"Yes, sir."

His eyebrows rose in carefully articulated surprise. "You amaze me. I thought only members of staff had keys to the building."

"Yes, sir. It's just that Mr Carr let me have one so I could use the computers when I needed."

"Mr Carr," he repeated ruminatively, and clucked his tongue against the roof of his mouth in disapproval. "I think we'd better have a word with him now, don't you?"

Before Zoe could give an opinion he had picked up the phone. "Hello, Sandra. Sorry to bother you again . . . Yes it is, isn't it? I should like to see Mr Carr. Would you mind getting a message to him? Oh, and perhaps you'd see if another member of staff could take over his lesson for ten minutes . . ."

He busied himself with some paperwork and Zoe was left standing uncomfortably till Mr Carr arrived two minutes later, looking flustered and apprehensive. The three of them stood in an awkward triangle. Zoe wanted no part of this but, for now, she had no choice.

"This young lady," Mr Jeal remarked, "tells me that she has lost a key to the computer room, and that you were going to come and see me about it. I don't recall your paying me a visit yesterday." It wasn't a question but it needed an answer.

Mr Carr cursed his luck. Under pressure, he had a habit of burying his head in the sand. Sometimes it worked; that was why he had delayed seeing the Senior Master. On other occasions, such as now, it failed spectacularly.

"I intended to see you yesterday," he managed at last, "but I was teaching all day."

Mr Jeal nodded smilingly at Zoe. "Thank you," he said. "You can go now."

As Zoe passed Mr Carr, she gave him what she hoped was a supportive glance. It occurred to her that she had just handed Mr Jeal his head on a plate.

The day ticked by. Teachers moved from quiet to chaos and back to the staffroom; pupils worked or refused to work; desks scraped in the classrooms and feet thundered up and down noisy flights of stairs. All this was regulated by the school bell.

For Mr Carr, that welcome ringing which marked the end of the day could not come soon enough. He had only to remember those ten excruciating minutes spent in the company of Mr Jeal to feel profoundly sick; ten minutes of subtle threats and promises. No — Mr Jeal would not inform the Headmaster as yet: presumably Mr Carr wouldn't mind helping him to supervise late detentions, or supporting Mr Jeal's campaign to become staff representative on the Board of Governors. And as for the key, well, it had probably been thrown away by now; they wouldn't have known what it was for anyway. "Yes," he'd said, "I think we can keep it as our little secret."

Had Hitler's henchmen ever felt as he did now, Mr Carr wondered. Blackmail was certainly a surer guarantee of loyalty than the fickle ties of friendship could produce. He was appalled at the speed with which he had conceded to all these polite, but undeniable, requests.

But worse than this was a stubborn ache in his mind. He could not put it into words: it was a feeling he had never experienced before. Had he done so, he would have recognised it for what it was: a premonition of disaster.

3.30 p.m.

So now they go home. Everyone else but me. My time's just begun.

4.45 p.m.

The place sounds so empty. Everyone out of the building, apart from the cleaning ladies of course. OK so far. Moving place to place; keeping one step ahead. Stop. Voices. Quiet, though. Far enough away. Some of the cleaners in the History room having their tea break? Check watch. Yes. Began five minutes ago. They'll be there for another ten. Keep moving. Damn! Why do these trainers squeak so much on the polished floor? Calm down. No hurry. So here's the door. Looks different somehow. Part of a different world; alien. Key. Lock. Click. So easy, but exciting too. Swinging open like that, as if it was oiled specially for me. Inviting me in. Close the door. Smooth; quiet. Good. Now for the difficult part. Because you know you've got to hold on till the right time, don't you?

God, it's weird in here. Like a murderer sitting in a room with all his victims lined up and waiting.

Waiting. Why is it that the worst part is always the waiting?

6.00 p.m.

That's the last of the blinds pulled down. Better to do it now: don't want the lights showing later. And I'm not going to do it in the dark. The dark is for criminals.

6.30 p.m.

I remember when I was seven, I went to a party. Boy at school with a lot of money — his parents lived in a huge house. After tea we played hide-and-seek. I was the first to go and hide; ended up in a big bedroom. By the wardrobe was an empty linen basket. I hid in there and waited.

Nobody came, not for a long while, then I heard footsteps on the stairs, voices outside the room. I wished I'd chosen somewhere else: somewhere I could breathe. Then they were in the room and I could hear them looking under the bed. Through the tiny gaps in the wickerwork basket I could see the tartan of a girl's skirt as she walked past.

And for a moment I wanted to give myself up.

6.50 p.m.

Where is he? He should be on his way by now. Listen for the keys jangling. That should be the first sign. It twists your nerves listening to nothing.

What was that? A door. The double door at the end of the corridor. And now? Yes, the keys. He's moving slowly — checking the doors further along. He won't try this one. He'll know just by looking that it's shut and locked. But what if he needs to open it for some other reason? What the hell am I going to say to him, sitting here in the half-dark like this?

He's closer now. I can hear his footsteps.

He's outside. Keep walking. Go on. Keep on walking!

And he has. As simple as that. Amazing.

OK, just a little while longer. Give him time to disappear. Not too long, though, because in another ten minutes the alarms will be on and then you'll be in real trouble. Count sixty, then it's time for the lights. Get a good look at the enemy. There's nothing they can do to stop you now.

Fifty, forty-nine, forty-eight.

Do you feel strong? Can you smash them all in five minutes? That's the most you can give yourself. Five only. Twenty monitors in five minutes. Four a minute. It's like a maths problem: if it takes five minutes to smash twenty computers, how long will it take to find out who did it?

Thirty, twenty-nine.

Unzip the bag. Take out the crowbar. Put it on the table — quietly! Remember when you go out through the window to shut it properly. Then there'll be no alarms. No-one to find out till the morning.

Stop it. Don't think ahead. One step at a time.

Time. Time. How much longer? I've lost count, but it doesn't matter now —

Click. Lights flicker.

Time to get down to business.

Wednesday

Since his arrival in the car park, when the caretaker had cornered him with the dreadful news, Mr Jeal had been embroiled in the affair of the wrecked computer room. At the moment he was seated at his desk, examining a list of names and feigning concern. There were many other jobs which required his attention, but the Head had placed him firmly in the front line and he had every intention of being seen to do his duty.

The list of possible suspects from the fourth and fifth year was compact but interesting. They were all of them trouble-makers. It would do them good to sweat.

He checked a timetable to find the whereabouts of the boy whose name headed the list, and typed a brief message for the relevant teacher. A passing child was halted, then sent scurrying off to a new destination. Adjusting his character to that of police inspector, Mr Jeal sat back at his desk and waited.

The Police themselves had obviously been informed and had arrived ceremoniously in a large car, attracting speculation on the part of the pupils and fuelling rumour. Having examined, photographed and dusted here and there for fingerprints, they had left equally ceremoni-ously, jostled by a crowd of curious youngsters, and were now sifting evidence and pursuing their own enquiries.

As the intruder had opened the computer room door with a key, they were also waiting for the school to come up with something. There were no signs of forced entry on the outside, nor had the alarm system been triggered. The only sign that anyone had been there, apart from the smashed computers, was a single open window.

All this made the Headmaster extremely uncomfort-able. His agitation was not helped by a sudden loud rap on his office door.

"Yes?" he said sharply.

There was no answer, so he strode to the door and flung it open. "What do you want?"

"I'm sorry for interrupting you." It was a sixth form girl. She blushed slightly and lowered her head. "I must have knocked harder than I meant to."

The Head immediately softened. "That's all right, but I'm rather busy at the moment with this — er — unfortunate incident."

"You mean the computers, sir?"

The Head groaned inwardly. Did the whole school know already? But perhaps that was inevitable. "That's right. What did you want to see me about, though?"

"Well, it's about that, actually. I thought I'd better come and explain something to you."

The Head looked confused. Zoe waited patiently until he realised it was too important to talk about in the corridor.

"Ah yes," he said finally. "Come in for a moment."

Gary was fourth on the list. He had been waiting outside Mr Jeal's room for twenty minutes already and was in the mood for a fight. The door opened and the previous candidate emerged looking subdued. Mr Jeal's head appeared.

"Ah, Gary. Sorry to have kept you waiting." He motioned him inside, and gestured towards a chair. "Sit down," he beamed.

Gary thought for a moment then sat.

"Now," Mr Jeal continued. "This shouldn't take long."

"Took you long enough with Adrian Young. I've been waiting nearly half an hour out there."

Mr Jeal looked at his watch with a rigid smile. "Nineteen minutes, actually, Gary. And I wouldn't advise you to start like that."

"Like what?" Gary glared at the little rotund man in his ill-fitting tweed jacket.

"Please yourself. I can be as pleasant or as unpleasant as you like. Personally, I'd like to keep things as friendly as possible."

Gary did not reply.

"Right then." Mr Jeal settled himself comfortably in his chair, then cocked his head ruminatively to one side. "Why did you do it, Gary?"

Gary's mouth opened slowly. "You what?"

"Let's not waste time. I've spoken to several people already this morning and all the evidence points to you."

"What the hell are you talking about?"

"I think you know perfectly well." Allowing no time for an answer, Mr Jeal continued: "For one thing, I'm sure you remember a conversation we had about a year and a half ago."

If he did, Gary showed no signs of recognition. He looked simply puzzled.

"Let me remind you then. Because you had managed to get yourself put down a class by your own ridiculous behaviour, and because you had already fallen into bad habits of work, it fell to me to inform you that you were no longer eligible to choose Computer Studies as an option."

"Yeah!" Gary was scornful. "What you mean is Carr had it in for me."

"*Mr* Carr, as teacher in charge of the subject, was simply making a reasonable decision. In his place I would have done the same thing." Mr Jeal looked strangely triumphant. "But I see you remember a little more of what happened now," he said. "And obviously you still have a very large chip on your shoulder about the way you feel you were treated. Isn't that true?"

The muscles in Gary's jaw began to work convulsively, but he said nothing. Mr Jeal walked round to where this insolent boy sat so dismissively silent. Standing, he was just above the level of Gary's head. "What better way to get your own back — " he measured his words precisely "— than to destroy the machines you were not allowed to work with."

He stared into the boy's eyes. The eyes always gave them away. He had expected to see panic in them; instead anger and a glint of pure hatred met his gaze.

"You berk!" Gary spat. "You think . . ."

"I *know*, Gary. Your eyes give you away: guilt written all over them."

"You must be joking!" Gary was on his feet now, and the difference in size between the two of them was suddenly very clear. "You don't know what you're talking about."

"No?" Mr Jeal sneered. "Sour grapes because you felt left out? You could have faced up to Mr Carr personally, of course, but then he's a man. You had to do it the cowardly way, didn't you?"

"You bastard!" Gary had grabbed him by the lapels before he could get back behind his desk. "I'm no coward. I could sort you out."

Beneath his mask of disgust, Mr Jeal looked worried. "Let go of me," he hissed. "You're only making things worse for yourself."

Gary hesitated, then pushed the older man away and turned to leave.

"And I shall want to see you later," Mr Jeal called. "In the Headmaster's room."

Gary's fists clenched and unclenched, and the muscles in his broad shoulders tautened. Then he stormed out.

Mr Jeal composed himself and ushered in the final candidate.

Zoe surveyed a potted plant in the corner of the room and waited for the Headmaster's reaction.

"Let me get this straight," he said, pushing back a strand of grey hair that had fallen over his forehead. "You say Mr Carr gave you a key to the computer room several months ago."

"Yes, sir. It was so I could get ahead with my work: I don't have the facilities at home."

"Quite. Yet I was not informed. And you also say that you lost this key on Monday of this week. Today is Wednesday and not a word of this has reached me till now."

"Oh, but I did tell a member of staff, sir. Two in fact."

The Headmaster looked very weary. He breathed heavily and rubbed a hand across his eyes. "Which members of staff did you inform?"

Zoe ticked off each event in the palm of her hand. "Well, first of all I told Mr Carr and he told me I should report it to Mr Jeal."

"And you told Mr Jeal how you came to lose it?"

"I didn't exactly lose it, sir. That's the point. I kept it in my purse, you see, and during registration on Monday someone took the purse from my bag."

The Head began to look desperate. "And what did Mr Jeal say when you told him it had been stolen?"

"He told me to check at home and it would probably turn up."

The Head's eyes rolled imploringly upwards.

"And it did," she continued. "The purse, that is. One of the cleaning ladies found it in a bin on Monday evening. Mr Jeal gave it back to me yesterday. But the money in it had gone, and so had the key."

Zoe looked at her shoes. "I'm sorry, sir. I feel it's partly my fault. Maybe I should have come to see you straight away."

The Head brushed an imaginary fly from somewhere near his forehead. "No, no — you're not to blame."

There was a knock at the door. He rose stiffly. "Thank you for coming to see me," he said. He opened the door for her, to find the ebullient figure of Mr Jeal smiling at him, his hand raised to knock a second time. Behind him hovered Mr Carr. He was twisting his straggling beard abstractedly. There was dandruff on his shirt-front, Zoe noticed as she passed him.

"Come in, gentlemen," she heard the Headmaster say, and his voice had acquired a new cutting edge.

Ten minutes later the bell went for the end of morning school. It was a different Mr Jeal who, shortly afterwards, left the Headmaster's room and fumed his way through a gaggle of hungry children on the path to his office.

"Sir?" A small girl approached him with half a dinner ticket clutched in one hand, and a tear-stained friend in the other.

"Not now, girl. I'm busy."

This was not so different from the way he had swept aside Zoe Charters and her lost purse earlier in the week, but the irony would have escaped him. He had just been hauled over the coals and he was angry. Mr Carr would suffer for it later.

He turned away from the crestfallen children and glimpsed the back of Gary Deakin disappearing round a corner. His rage needed an outlet. "Deakin," he called. "Gary Deakin!" And he sprinted after the vanishing figure, keys jangling in his pockets as he ran.

He caught up with the hurrying boy by the school drive. "I'd like to speak to you for a minute," he panted, unused to such sudden exertion.

"It's my dinnertime, if you don't mind."

Mr Jeal forced himself to sound generous. "Look, I think we were both a bit hasty earlier. Just come to my office for a moment and let's sort it out."

"That's what you said last time." Gary shrugged half-heartedly. "Five minutes, then I'm off."

"Fine." Mr Jeal steered him amicably by the arm back towards his office.

Outside, among the other pupils, Mr Jeal had felt exposed, vulnerable. Once the door was closed, he was safe again on home ground. "Well, it's very simple," he began. "I'd like you to empty your pockets."

"I don't believe it." Gary looked amazed.

"Something to hide?"

"Oh, for crying out loud . . ." He dredged a hand into the left pocket of his overcoat, and removed a dirty handkerchief which he dangled between two fingers. "All right? Can I go now?"

"When you've shown me what's inside the other one."

Mr Jeal waited. This was all a charade, but if the boy was guilty — and Mr Jeal felt in his bones that he was — then putting pressure on him now might pay dividends later. Come to think of it, it would be worth getting another key cut. Easy enough matter to drop it in Deakin's pocket at the right moment. Pity he hadn't thought of it before, really.

"Well, come on then," he said.

"You just don't give up, do you?" Gary plunged his hand into the other pocket. "Empty, see?"

He pulled out the lining just to make the point. As he did so, something fell from its folds and chimed as it hit the floor. He stared down in disbelief.

Mr Jeal could barely conceal his joy, but contented himself with a raised eyebrow.

"At last," he murmured. "Thank you, Gary."

At the far end of the corridor was Mrs Mallory's room. She was the Deputy Head and specialised in friendly conversations with the girls about their personal problems. Her room was more homely than either of her colleagues'; pictures from the Art room adorned the walls and cuddly toys from Needlework groups mingled on top of her cupboards. She was just about to close the door and enjoy her packed lunch, when Zoe Charters' face appeared outside.

"Yes, Zoe. What is it?"

The girl appeared very put-out. She seemed lost for words.

"Is it serious, dear?"

"Yes, Mrs Mallory. I . . ." Again she lapsed into uncomfortable silence.

Mrs Mallory's maternal instincts triumphed over her hunger. "Well, if it won't take too long . . ." Zoe came in tentatively and closed the door, and Mrs Mallory pulled down the Do not disturb blind.

The Headmaster's face wore a gentler expression. He was pouring his second sherry. "Er, another one for you, Maurice?"

Mr Jeal held up his arm as if stopping traffic. "No thank you, Headmaster." He laughed. "Not while I'm on duty."

The Head looked at his watch. "Hm. The Police should be here soon. Where's the boy now?"

"In my office. Mr Trump is with him."

"Ah." The Head seemed reassured: Mr Trump played rugby for the county. "I must say," he mused, "it seems remarkably stupid of the boy to keep the key on his person."

"True, Headmaster, but I put it down to the lad's arrogance. At any rate, we'd have found him out sooner or later. After all," he laughed again heartily, "I already had him down as my key suspect!"

"I don't believe it." Mrs Mallory leaned back in her chair and shook her head.

Zoe smiled apologetically. "I know it's a shock, Mrs Mallory, but I'm afraid it's the truth."

The Deputy Head looked down at her ashtray as if wrestling with her conscience, then reached into the nearest desk drawer and removed a packet of cigarettes and a lighter. "Three days I've been off these damned things," she said, "and now I'm back where I started."

She walked round to Zoe's side of the desk, propped herself on the edge and pulled the ashtray across. "I think you'd better start at the beginning."

"I don't really know where the beginning is, but how would it be if I started a few months ago?"

Mrs Mallory's expression of concern evaporated. "Don't be frivolous!" she snapped. "I just want to know what on earth possessed you."

She paused, then as there was no reply, asked again: "Why did you do it?"

"No." Zoe turned and gazed at an orange elephant on top of the filing cabinet.

"I beg your pardon?"

"I won't tell you why I did it, but if you sit down for a minute — " She gestured to a spare seat " — I'll tell you *how*."

Being treated as an inferior in her own office was a new experience for Mrs Mallory. More in surprise than obedience she sat.

"I managed to persuade Mr Carr to let me have a key to the room months ago," Zoe continued. "Then I started to stay behind. I spent some time on the computer of course, but mainly I was working out what time people came and went. I figured it couldn't be that difficult. I mean, if prisoners of war can get past guard dogs, searchlights and machine-guns, then getting in and out of school ought to be straightforward enough. Mind you, there were a few tricky moments; smuggling in a crowbar and keeping it hidden all day wasn't easy. My locker was too small to hide it in so I had to lug it around with me. By the end of the day I felt like I'd been weight-training for six hours."

Zoe warmed to her storytelling. It took her only five minutes to recount the rest of the day's activities. Her voice was calm and level, her tone entirely matter-of-fact. She could have been discussing the weather or the relative merits of back- or slip-stitch. Having dispensed with the previous day, she turned to the present.

"Today, when everyone was fussing and whispering, I took the time off from joining in to listen for a while. Who was getting the blame? Gary Deakin. I wasn't surprised. He was an obvious culprit. So, while he was getting the third degree, I found his coat in the cloakroom and deposited the key safely in his pocket. After I'd made a song and dance about losing it, it was a fair bet they'd start searching people sooner or later. It just happened to be sooner."

Zoe sat back in the chair and crossed her legs. "That's about all there is." She shrugged her shoulders and waited.

There was a long pause. Mrs Mallory closed her eyes, then opened them again and fixed Zoe with a cold stare. "If this is true," she said quietly and steadily, "and at the moment I'm still saying *if* — then why did you come and tell me?"

"Conscience?" Zoe suggested.

Mrs Mallory remained impassive. "You tell me."

"Well, yes, I suppose it was in a way. Originally, I'd thought of forcing the computer room door to make it look like the work of a complete outsider, but then how would they have got into the building in the first place without setting off the alarms? So it had to be someone in the school. That way I could also use the key to

148

incriminate them and keep myself in the clear. Everyone thinks I lost it two days ago.

"I hadn't planned it would be Gary. It didn't seem to matter who it was; it was just the last part of a clever idea. But when I saw him out there, waiting — they've called the Police, haven't they? — I decided. I couldn't let him suffer for something he doesn't even know about."

"Very noble of you!"

"I know you're being sarcastic," Zoe continued unperturbed, "but I think I probably am. After all, I didn't have to come and tell you."

"No," Mrs Mallory mused. "Then again, your story, convincing though I must admit it is, could be a complete pack of lies."

Zoe looked shocked. "What on earth would I do that for?"

"I don't know. To protect Gary maybe, if you knew he'd done it?"

"Huh." Zoe's voice was contemptuous. "I might feel guilty about what's happened to him but I'm not that noble. He's no friend of mine and if he had done it, he'd deserve whatever he got."

"And what about you?"

"What *about* me?"

"I shall have to tell the Headmaster and he will inform the Police. What will you do then?"

Zoe beamed at Mrs Mallory with a smile that would have disarmed her worst enemy. "Simple," she said. "I shall deny everything I've just told you."

Mrs Mallory gave every appearance of someone who, without any warning, has had both feet kicked out from under her. "You what?" she spluttered.

"I'll say you made it all up." As Mrs Mallory seemed unwilling or unable to reply she continued, "Look, I reckon the whole thing should be dropped. You could convince the Head to do that."

"Are you out of your mind? What possible reason . . . ?"

Zoe's voice was still matter-of-fact. "First, there's no case against me, so you're wasting your time if you try to prove I did it. I doubt if the Head would believe you anyway. If, on the other hand, he has Gary prosecuted, I'll wait until the case comes up and *then* I'll confess. Not to the Police, but to any newspaper that wants the story. You'd all look pretty silly then.

"And while I'm telling them that, there are a few more stories I've got up my sleeve. For example, Mr Hamilton runs the photography club and you should hear some of the things the fifth year girls say about what goes on in the darkroom."

Mrs Mallory was slowly changing colour.

"And as you know," Zoe breezed on, "at least six married members of staff have had affairs since I've been at this school, two of them on a school trip in front of the pupils. I was on that trip, as it happens, *and* I had a camera. Interestingly enough, one of the others has the key to the medical room which not only has a comfortable bed . . ."

"Zoe!" Mrs Mallory exploded. "You can't get away with this."

"Why not?" Zoe grinned. "I won't say anything I can't prove, which is more than you can do. You said yourself, *my* story could be a pack of lies. It's all too improbable: academic girl, with a promising life ahead of her, smashing up computers. You can't pin it on me unless I confess; I'll only confess if Gary goes to court: if I do confess, the school is going to get some very bad publicity. Admit it; every way you lose."

A look of despair, then sadness crossed Mr Mallory's face. "And you? Do you lose nothing?"

"Well, if the worst comes to the worst, at least I'll make a few pennies from the Press."

"I'm serious, Zoe. Maybe you don't care, at the moment, but what about your parents? Think how it will affect them."

Zoe's expression suddenly changed. She was very, very angry. She gritted her teeth then said slowly, "Don't try using my parents to make me feel guilty. You know nothing about my parents." She glared at the older woman. "Nothing at all."

Mrs Mallory backed off. There seemed little room for bargaining. "If I'm to go through with this charade," she said at last, "won't you at least tell me the reason for it all?"

"You mean my motive."

Mrs Mallory nodded.

Zoe stood up and walked to the door.

"No," she said, flicked up the blind, opened the door and left.

The two policemen cast faintly amused looks at each other. "I beg your pardon, sir?" said the senior of them.

Having just emerged from a hurried consultation in his room, the Head was visibly flustered. "There has been a slight mistake, I'm afraid. We believed we had the culprit when we contacted you, but it now seems clear that we were wrong. We had been given . . . misleading information."

The senior officer replaced his notebook with an air of deliberation. "I see."

"Yes — an irresponsible prank. Some of the unfortunate boy's friends found it funny to . . . er . . ."

"Set him up," the younger policeman volunteered.

"Precisely. We shall of course be dealing with them most severely. I regret you've been inconvenienced in this way," he added. "It was only fortunate we discovered our mistake before you arrived."

The officer caught a tang of sherry in the air. "Absolutely, sir. You will keep us informed if there are any other developments?"

"Of course, of course. We shall be doing our utmost, I can assure you." With an attempt at renewing confidence, he shook both men firmly by the hand and retired to the sanctuary of the secretary's office.

Anyone passing a secluded bench on the north side of town that evening would have seen two people in quiet conversation. Not that they would have been likely to take much notice, assuming most probably that the teenage boy and girl were another young couple looking for a quiet place to be romantic. Romance, however, was not what brought them together. Indeed, they had not spoken to each other for six months, apart from one brief telephone call earlier in the week.

It was the boy who spoke first. "You're amazing, do you know that?"

"Just determined." Zoe stretched her arms behind her head. "This is the first time I've relaxed all week."

Gary was reflective. "They could still change their minds."

"They might, but I meant what I said. I've got plenty of material for embarrassing them. I've been collecting it for a long time — ever since I worked out the plan."

"How long ago was that?" Gary asked. "You never told me."

"No, I didn't, did I? Maybe I've been too cautious with you, but I reckoned that would be safer for both of us."

"Will you tell me now?" he persisted.

"Why not. Altogether, it's been three years."

Gary whistled. "That long?"

He paused. "I feel nervous asking you things; I don't know why . . ."

"But? Go on. Ask me. You won't get another chance, and I know I can trust you. You've proved that."

"But that's it. Why trust me in the first place? How come you picked me out? As a matter of fact, I still don't really understand why you needed me at all."

"Oh, Gary." She moved closer and put her arm on his. "I have been rotten to you, haven't I? Do you feel used?" She looked rueful. "You should do. If anyone's been trusting it's you. Waiting for the Police like that: you must have wondered if I'd deserted you at the last minute."

"I was sweating a bit."

"I'm sorry. I think I was enjoying myself a bit too much with Mrs Mallory. But I needed someone who could stand the pressure — who wouldn't crack at the last minute. That's why I chose you, Gary."

"But why use anyone else at all? What was the point of making things so complicated if you could get away with it by yourself?"

"Because there was more to it than just breaking up bits of machinery and 'getting away with it'." Traces of anger had crept into her previously calm voice. "I wanted them to look the idiots they are: teachers who talk to you about the world outside when most don't even live in it themselves. I wanted to be able to tell them, to show I wasn't scared or ashamed of what I'd done and know they could do nothing about it."

She sighed. "I needed you to bargain with. Does that sound dreadful?"

Gary weighed this up carefully. He seemed about to say something, but ran his hand along the back of the bench instead.

Zoe smiled at him affectionately. "Go on," she said.

"I was going to ask you a question."

"Well?"

Gary shrugged. "Maybe I shouldn't. Some things are private, aren't they?"

"Who said you were a thug?" Zoe punched his arm. "Would you walk off if I said I thought you were sensitive and thoughtful?"

"No."

"I know you wouldn't. But some people can only see what's in front of them. That's why you're a thug and a moron, and I'm a nice, respectable girl."

Gary laughed.

"But I'm not nice and respectable. People who are get stamped on, and no-one's doing that to me. Listen, Gary. Some day, maybe, you'll meet my dad. Probably not, though, so let me describe him to you. He's a quiet, middle-aged man. I don't think he's ever been young, except in photographs. He was trained to use his hands, with clocks and watches. It was a dying profession even then but he struggled on, into the age of the self-winding watch and electric alarm clock. He enjoyed his work, mind you, and he was losing money hand over fist before he decided he'd got to change his job. He was in his late thirties by then.

"After a lot of searching he finally got a job in a car factory, on the assembly line. Fair enough, it was boring and he had to travel two hours every day, but it paid the rent. Then came the new machinery: one man could do the work of ten. So he was made redundant.

"That was five years ago, and since I was twelve I've watched him sliding down. First he tried to get a similar job, then any job: but who needs a middle-aged man when there are young people out of work?

"Am I sounding too bitter?" A distant look clouded over her eyes, and when she spoke again it was barely a whisper.

"The arguments came next. Two people who loved each other suddenly shouting and fighting. My mother walked out. She came back, when he begged her to; now they don't even talk to each other. I live with strangers."

For a time it seemed she had finished. Then, with her old fire, she said, "I suppose something snapped in me when we were all told, in the third year, how we could be sure of a job in this technological world if only we trained with computers. And everyone else was lapping it up. They were being fed dreams: work out a new computer game and make millions. They couldn't see that they'd end up as bits of machinery themselves. When they're not needed to push the buttons any more, what will they do with their training then?"

Gary took a deep breath. "I know what you mean," he said quietly.

"But — ?" she prompted.

"Well, it's not really the machines, is it? It's the way we use them."

"Maybe. Anyhow, I've finished. I'm not planning to fight progress single-handed or anything like that. I've had a small piece of private revenge. That'll do me."

There was a long silence.

"When things have cooled down," Gary ventured, "could I . . . I mean, maybe we could see each other again."

"No."

Gary looked away.

"Don't get me wrong," she said. "I like you but — " a broad smile suddenly flashed across her face " — it would never do. A respectable boy like you and a trouble-maker like me. What would people say?"

She was gone before he had a chance to reply.